I could not save Mahatma Gandhi

Untold Stories from a Witness's Diary

I could not save Mahatma Gandhi

Untold Stories from a Witness's Diary

Dr Jagdishchandra Jain

Compiled by James Campbell

frontpage

frontpage
www.frontpagepublications.com

First published 2010
First reprint 2018

FRONTPAGE PUBLICATIONS LIMITED
Level 2, 13 John Prince's Street, London W1G 0JR, United Kingdom

Frontpage
Level B, 76 B B Ganguly Street, Kolkata 700012, India

ISBN 978 81 908841 3 6

Typeset by Compuset International
85 Park Street, Kolkata 700016

In ever loving memory of
Prof Dr Jagdishchandra Jain
and
Smt Kamalshri Jain

Preface and Acknowledgment

In independent India, the greatest tragedy was the assassination of the Father of the Nation, Mohandas Karamchand Gandhi, who was adorned with the title of *Mahatma*, by Gurudev Rabindranath Tagore. It is indeed history's greatest irony that the *Mahatma*, the Great Soul, who was the architect of India's struggle for freedom, from two hundred years of colonial rule, had to sacrifice his life at the hands of his own countrymen.

It is even more heartbreaking that Gandhi, an apostle of peace, who had introduced the unique strategy of *satyagraha*, the only weapon for the oppressed to combat tyranny through non-violent resistance, was the target of a well-hatched conspiracy.

Dr Jagdishchandra Jain, my late father, based in Bombay (now Mumbai, India), came to know of the plot to assassinate Mahatma Gandhi, much in advance, from Madanlal Pahwa, one of the key conspirators. He instantaneously informed the Bombay Government. Instead of acting on this vital lead, the authorities, unfortunately, took their own time in passing on this information and the misfortune struck on 30 January 1948 when the Father of the Nation was eventually assassinated.

My father regularly maintained his daily diary; the day when Madanlal had confided in him of the conspiracy, the day when he had approached the authorities to alert them, the manner in which he was humiliated in turn at almost every stage in his lone battle to save the life of Mahatma Gandhi and the days he spent in Delhi as the Chief Prosecution Witness in the Gandhi Murder Trial. Much to his anguish, even after risking his own life and endangering the security of our entire family, my father could not save the Mahatma. This was his everlasting regret, until he breathed his last.

We are indebted to our family friend James Campbell, a young, enthusiastic journalist, who had volunteered to undertake the arduous task of preparing the manuscript from the dog-eared pages of the diary for its publication.

We owe an appreciation to *frontpage*, the Publishers, who have ensured at every step to produce a quality publication for our readers around the world, many of whom might not be aware of the untold story behind the greatest conspiracy that shook the world 62 years back.

15 March 2010   Anil Jagdishchandra Jain

Mohandas Karamchand Gandhi

Jawaharlal Nehru

Sardar Vallabhbhai Patel

Maulana Abul Kalam Azad

Morarji Desai

Mohammad Ali Jinnah

Huseyn Shaheed Suhrawardy

Lord Mountbatten

A group photo of people accused in the Mahatma Gandhi's Murder case.
Standing: Shankar Kistaiya, Gopal Godse, Madanlal Pahwa, Digamber Badge
(approver). Sitting: Narayan Apte, Vinayak D Savarkar, Nathuram Godse,
Vishnu Karkare.

Gandhi Murder Trial at Red Fort, Delhi, 22 June 1948.
Front row (left to right): Nathuram Godse, Apte, Karkare
Middle row (left to right): Badge (approver), Madanlal, Gopal Godse
Back row (left to right): Shankar Kistaiya, Savarkar and Parchure.

The Statesman

PUBLISHED SIMULTANEOUSLY FROM CALCUTTA AND DELHI

MAHATMA SHOT DEAD

Maratha Hindu Said To Be Assailant

GANDHIJI'S BODY TO BE CREMATED TODAY

Day Of Mourning For Entire World, Says Mountbatten

Calcutta's De Sorrow

Public Activiti Suspended

London Stirred By Tragedy

Homage By Eminent Britons

The Sunday
Amrita Bazar Patrika

NDIA WEEPS—WORLD WEEPS
UMANITY'S HOMAGE TO NOBLEST SOUL

SOBBING MASS JOIN GREAT ONE'S LAST JOURNEY

TOUCHING FUNERAL SCENES IN DELHI

NEW DELHI, Jan 31.—At 4-55 P. M. to-day the funeral pyre of Mahatma Gandhi was lit by his third son, Ramdas Gandhi, in the presence of at least half-a-million mourners.

Mahatma's body was carried from the bier by the Ashramites and placed on the sandalwood pyre with the head to the North. Flowers, Khadi-garlands and wreaths were placed at the feet of the Mahatma. The first wreath was placed by Dr. Lo, the Chinese Ambassador. The National Flag that covered the bier was removed and sandalwood war piled upon the body.

Priest, Pandit Ram Dhan Sharma, recited from Vedic texts while Ramdas Gandhi

'If I am to die by the bullet of a mad man, I must do so smiling. There must be no anger within me. God must be in my heart and on my lips.'

Mohandas K Gandhi
28 January 1948,
two days prior to his assassination

I could not save Mahatma Gandhi

Prologue

On 21 January 1948, early in the morning I was almost awake under a warm woollen blanket when suddenly I heard someone screaming 'bomb blast in Delhi!, bomb blast in Delhi!' I peeped through the window to find the newspaper boy shouting, 'Gandhiji is in trouble'. I ran out and snatched the paper from his hand even before he could throw it at my doorstep.

I read the headlines and the blood froze in my veins.

'Bomb Explodes at Gandhi's Prayer Meeting in Delhi.'

I was stunned. Sitting in Bombay, more than 800 miles away from Delhi, India's capital, I realised all that Madanlal had told me was true.

It was an irony that Mohandas Karamchand Gandhi, who led India's struggle for freedom from two hundred years of colonial rule, was facing threats to his life from his own countrymen. An apostle of peace, who taught the oppressed the new philosophy of *satyagraha*, a powerful weapon of combating tyranny through the non-violent means of mass civil disobedience, had just faced a brutal attack on his life. How can we imagine Mahatma, the great soul, being killed by a misguided group of people prompted by vested interests? No. I must act fast to avert any further mischief and save *Bapu*, our beloved Father of the Nation.

Before I could think any further, a voice said, 'You were right Professor.' I turned around and saw Angad Singh, my walk partner at Shivaji Park, hurrying towards me. Usually, we met at the park.

'We must contact the authorities now.' Angad was emphatic, 'There is no time to waste!'

We tried Sardar Vallabhbhai Patel, the then Deputy Prime Minister and in charge of Home Affairs, who we knew was in Bombay only to be told that he had already left for the airport and his flight would take off in the next fifteen minutes. Our attempt to establish contact with S K Patil, the then President of the Bombay Provincial Congress Committee also proved futile as Patil had accompanied Sardar.

I was feeling helpless and my blood pressure was rising as I started sweating in that winter morning. 'I must save *Bapu*, come what may!' I resolved.

After several frustrating attempts, B G Kher, the then Premier of the Government of Bombay, answered my frantic calls and gave me an appointment to see him at the Secretariat at 4.00 pm. I was relieved assuming that in the next few hours I would get the opportunity to lighten my burden and divulge all the information that Madanlal had given me.

⁂

Madanlal, the hapless refugee

It was on 26 October 1947 when Madanlal came to see me. Madanlal Kishanlal Pahwa, a fair-complexioned, tall and well-built young boy of around 22 years with a healthy moustache, was a refugee displaced from Pakpattan in the district of Montgomery, now in Pakistan. After the Partition, since August 1947, this Punjabi youth had been languishing in the Chembur Refugee Camp in Bombay. I first met him at this relief camp which was sponsored by the University.

Madanlal had served the Royal Indian Navy as a Wireless Operator stationed in Bombay and he knew the city quite well. After Partition, this was perhaps the main reason why he came to Bombay to look for a suitable employment.

I introduced Madanlal to my friends: 'Here is Madanlal, a forced migrant from Pakistan after the Partition. He has saved many lives; rescued women from being massacred. Now he is in Chembur camp, looking for a suitable job.' Visibly upset, Madanlal told us that he visited the Employment Exchange almost every day but in vain. He was now ready to take even peon's (menial's) job. Madanlal could not continue sitting idle; he would need something to occupy himself. Angad Singh suggested that he should think of selling vegetables rather than doing an aimless job at someone else's beck and call. He could take vegetables from Bassein to sell in Bombay but Madanlal instantly dismissed the idea since he had no money to start a business.

I made an offer to Madanlal which he most willingly accepted. He would collect books from me to sell which I would procure from the publishers at a discount of 25 per cent. Madanlal wanted to start this new venture from the very next day.

Next morning, as I returned from my daily round of morning exercise at Shivaji Park, I found Madanlal impatiently waiting for me. He immediately collected the books from me, and in turn, gave me a chit reading Madanlal, 162 Chembur Camp. Madanlal stepped into a new life.

The next morning Madanlal turned up again. It was, however, a different Madanlal; a confident man who had sold all the books in a suburban train. He cleared the dues and proudly asked for more books. For the next ten to twelve days, Madanlal followed a fixed schedule; he would come in the morning, settle the accounts, and take a new set of books.

As I came to know him better, Madanlal narrated a poignant tale of his life; he was just a month old when he lost his mother. His father Kashmiri Lal married again, but Madanlal found no parental love in the new family. In 1945, after passing his matriculation exam, Madanlal disappeared in search of a decent living. Kashmiri Lal was left with no clue, and only after a few months, he received a letter from his son telling him that he had joined the Royal Indian Navy in Bombay. Madanlal's tenure in the Navy was, however, short-lived since in 1946, after the Second World War, he was honourably discharged from service.

Madanlal's homecoming, however, put Kashmiri Lal in a fix. Worried about his son, Kashmiri Lal had met his old friend Sardar Tarlok Singh in July 1947. Tarlok was then one of the secretaries of Pandit Jawaharlal Nehru, chief of the Congress, the largest political party of India, and the *de facto* Prime Minister in the Viceroy's Executive Council, the cabinet of the government of British India headed by the Viceroy of India. Tarlok happily assured his friend a job of Assistant Sub-Inspector of Police for Madanlal.

Nobody knew that within a few days their lives would be turned upside down. In August 1947, following the Partition, many of the fleeing Hindu and Sikh refugees on the way to India from Pakistan lost their loved ones, and life-long savings at the hands of the murderous mobs. Besides forcible conversion, young girls were being abducted, women were being raped in front of their husbands and children, or their husbands were being slaughtered, leaving trains to arrive India laden with dead bodies.

Madanlal fled in his cousin's bus with all his belongings, clothes, gold, jewelleries and currency. In the name of *Jihad*, Pakistani soldiers on the way confiscated the bus and all that it contained. Madanlal entered India without even a coin on him but his ill luck did not stop there. He heard that while proceeding towards India his father was severely wounded beyond recognition in a train ambush near Ferozpur, a bordering town on the banks of the river Sutlej, and the old man was simply gasping his last at an overcrowded hospital. Madanlal had vowed in front of his father's mutilated body,

'I must take revenge – the Muslims should flee the way we had.'

༄

Madanlal enters a new world

Despite the shock and hurt of the Partition, Madanlal was making a success of his new life as a trader.

With the approach of Diwali, the *Festival of Lights*, celebrated by Hindus, Sikhs, and Jains, Madanlal decided to extend his book dealing business to firecrackers as well selling them from door to door and making a tidy sum in the process.

After this success, he decided to source limes from Ahmednagar, a city almost 200 miles away, to sell in Bombay but this adventure did not work out so well and he suffered losses. Taking some more books from me he decided to visit Ahmednagar again to make good of whatever loss he had made. He wrote one or two letters from Ahmednagar and promised to settle my dues on his return but I did not hear from him for a while.

I saw Madanlal again on 10 January 1948. Early in the morning just as I was about to go for my routine walk at Shivaji Park, I found him waiting outside with a muffler round his neck ostensibly trying to cover his face. He had a cane in his hand, which he would swish while talking to me in a low voice. Within seconds I noticed visible changes in his behaviour, carelessness in his attitude and arrogance in his eyes. I also spotted a middle-aged man, well built with sallow complexion and small, peculiar eyes keeping a close watch on Madanlal from a distance. Madanlal identified the man as his *seth* with whose help he had two fruit shops at Ahmednagar. Madanlal abruptly left only to catch me again after few minutes. I observed that he wanted to say something more but was evidently hesitant as his 'seth' was keeping a close watch on him.

After two or three days, Madanlal came again one afternoon when I was not home. My wife asked him how his life was going and Madanlal gave a surprising response.

'I have a good job at Ahmednagar. I get sufficient money. Moreover, thousands of volunteers are working for me. They respect me and the local police are under our control. You must have seen my photograph in the leading dailies.'

He continued, 'The other day when the Congress leader, Rao Saheb Patwardhan, started delivering his speech about Hindu-Muslim unity, I simply couldn't control myself. It is all because of Gandhi and his followers that we are in such a wretched condition now. We have lost everything for the Congress. I pulled that leader, held his collar and brought him down from the podium. I will show you the papers in which my photographs appeared.'

On the same day, it was about 8.00 pm, when I was waiting for the news broadcast from All India Radio, I saw Madanlal emerging with a bunch of newspapers in hand. Showing the newspapers, he boasted how he had held Rao Saheb Patwardhan by his neck and whipped out a knife to stab him. Police had intervened then to disperse the unruly mob and thus Rao Saheb was saved. Madanlal told me about his 'seth' whom I had seen accompanying him the other day. He was called Karkare and owned two hotels besides some fruit shops at Ahmednagar.

'Although I work for him,' Madanlal asserted, 'he looks after me.' He whispered, 'We have formed a party, collected lots of arms and ammunition which we have dumped in the jungle. We have driven away all the Muslim fruit vendors from Ahmednagar. Karkare is financing us and there is a warrant for his arrest but nothing will happen so long we have police on our side.

In Bombay also we have an arsenal.' Madanlal had been taken to the place blindfolded, and boasted that, 'the armoury is guarded by a Maharashtrian disguised as a Sikh.'

After a silence, Madanlal resumed, 'Recently, I was about to blow up the house of a rich Muslim there in Ahmednagar. Unfortunately, the police arrived just before the fuse could catch fire and neutralised the fuse.'

I reasoned that Madanlal developed such a violent and extreme temperament presumably because of his sufferings in Pakistan. Before embarking on any mission he would overtly boast about it. Madanlal confirmed that he was involved in the activities of Rashtriya Swayam-sevak Sangh (RSS), an extremist Hindu organisation, when he proudly announced, 'Barrister Savarkar is very happy with my deeds. The other day, he talked to me for nearly two hours. He patted me on my back and asked me to carry on.'

I was terribly disturbed. A disgruntled refugee gained the blessings of Vinayak Damodar Savarkar, a fierce critic of the Congress, and the central icon of the Hindu nationalist political ideology, *Hindutva*, with financial support from Karkare, a fanatic Maharashtrian —a fatal combination indeed.

After a few brief exchanges of information and political ideas, Madanlal elaborated some of his daring and *glorious* exploits, and slowly his attention veered to something 'yet-to-be-accomplished'! Madanlal finally disclosed the plot of eliminating a national leader whose name was, apparently, not known to him. I was not at all convinced with his arguments. With great persuasion, Madanlal ultimately confessed in a whisper, 'It is Gandhiji.'

I could not believe my ears. I could not believe that someone could even think of killing Bapu. I was distressed to see an innocent refugee being enticed to the heinous crime, perhaps for money. I sensed that someone was trying to exploit his feelings of hopelessness and loss after the Partition.

Madanlal started elaborating; a group of like-minded young men had been formed. At Birla House, Delhi where Bapu was camping, Madanlal would hurl a bomb at the prayer meeting of Gandhiji following which pandemonium would be created giving Madanlal's other associates the chance to attack Bapu.

I was horrified. 'Do you understand the implications of what you say?' I warned Madanlal. 'If you dare to take part in anything of that sort, rest assured, your life will be ruined.' We spent more than two hours at the seashore discussing the contributions of Mahatma Gandhi. Madanlal was initially vacillating, but I was certain, he would not discard altogether what I had told him for his own benefit.

I simply could not sleep until I shared my agony with Angad Singh, who I met the next morning.

'How can you believe him?' Angad Singh was not sure even after I reported my conversation with Madanlal verbatim.

'Nowadays, don't you know that all the refugees are openly cursing Gandhiji and Congress?' Angad perhaps tried to comfort me; he continued, 'Madanlal must have been allured by someone, poor fellow! You are talking about passing this information to the authorities. I am afraid, Professor, in that case, we might ourselves get into trouble. Let's pray to God that good sense prevails on the refugee boy.'

After a couple of days, on 15 January 1948, Madanlal came in a hurry to see me on his way to the railway station. 'I am going', Madanlal confirmed.

'Where?', I asked him.

'Delhi'

'Why?'

'Sir, I have got some urgent work over there,' Madanlal assured me.

〰

My first meeting with the Ministers

All through my journey to the Central Secretariat, Bombay, I was simply thinking of Madanlal. By the grace of God, Bapu had been saved from the bomb blast, but those devils might strike again.

I had recounted all that I had learnt from Madanlal to B G Kher, the then Premier of the Provincial Government of Bombay. During our discussion, Morarji Desai, the then Home Minister of the Bombay Province, appeared from the adjacent room. I was bent upon proving that this act of Madanlal should not be treated as an impulsive operation of a mad refugee. On the contrary, there was a well-knit conspiracy being hatched to eliminate the Father of the Nation. What I had gathered from Madanlal was that he would throw a bomb at the prayer meeting which would create chaos, and, taking advantage of the situation, Madanlal's associates would attack Gandhiji. Madanlal and his other accomplices had formed a party financed by one Karkare from Ahmednagar. Moreover, Savarkar had not only blessed the group, but also encouraged them to move forward. We would need to take proper precautionary measures to ensure that Mahatma would live long. I had also volunteered to go to Delhi, if required, and requested the Ministers to put me in contact with Madanlal, who was in police custody following his abortive attack on Gandhiji, so that I might extract more information about the conspiracy from him.

On that evening, Morarji Desai was leaving for Ahmedabad, then another important city in the state of Maharashtra, around 350 miles north of Bombay; Desai would convey whatever I had told him to Sardar Vallabhbhai Patel at Ahmedabad. A warrant to arrest Karkare was already issued, and the Home Minister viewed that if I had contacted him earlier, he would have got the conspirators arrested before they could leave Bombay. I had never taken Madanlal seriously, as it was beyond my imagination that anyone could ever think of killing Gandhiji!

I heaved a sigh of relief as soon as I stepped out of the secretariat. I was confident that the Government would now save Gandhiji.

⌒∾⌒

Before Independence

Independence came, but not for a united India. On 14 August 1947, the Union Jack which was ruling over India was split into two—a tricolour flag with the Asokan wheel in the middle and a green coloured flag with crescent and a star. National freedom ended up dividing the territory into India and Pakistan. Madanlal was not the solitary victim; more than twelve million people were forced to uproot themselves for fear of the future.

Communal strife on a scale never known before caused anguish and suffering that led to an end of an incalculable number who were shot, burnt, battered and tortured to death followed by an inevitable famine claiming lives, who had otherwise managed to survive the communal frenzy.

With the Second World War drawing to an end, the then Labour Government was elected to power in the United Kingdom in the general elections held in July 1945. In their pledged policy of social reform, appreciating the panoptic mood of the subcontinent starving for freedom, and greatly influenced by the US public opinion, the new regime favoured early self-government for India. Immediately after the surrender of Japan in the War, on 17 February 1946, Clement Attlee, the then Prime Minister of the United Kingdom, announced that a Cabinet Mission aimed to discuss and plans for the transfer of power from the British Raj to Indian leadership, providing India with independence under Dominion status in the Commonwealth of Nations, would soon meet both the mainstream political parties in India—the Congress, founded in 1885 and the Muslim League which came into existence later in 1906.

On 15 March 1946, Attlee's statement in the British House of Commons soliciting a new approach in the changed Indian scenario was a pragmatic step forward in resolving the political tension. A high-powered Cabinet Mission comprising Lord Pethick-Lawrence, Secretary of State for India, Sir Stafford Cripps, the President of the Board of Trade, and A V Alexander, the First Lord of the Admiralty reached India on 23 March 1946. Lord A P Wavell, the then Viceroy of India joined the team at Delhi on 2 April 1946.

In the Cabinet Mission Plan, a three-tier federation was proposed in India where provinces, groups and the centre would come up, and their implementation under the broad outline of the Plan would be left to the Constituent Assembly. While Nehru suggested conditional participation in the Constituent Assembly reserving the right to modify the Cabinet Mission Plan, Jinnah, the chief architect of Pakistan, recalled the Lahore Resolution of 22-24 March 1940 when the famous 'two-nation theory' was propounded and a demand for an independent sovereign state for the Muslim nation in India was put forward. In the March 1940 Lahore summit, Jinnah in his presidential address said,

'Islam and Hinduism are not religions in the strict sense of the word, but are in fact different and distinct social orders, and it is only a dream that Hindus and Muslims can ever evolve a common nationality. This misconception of one Indian nation has gone far beyond the limits and is the cause of most of our troubles and will lead India to destruction if we fail to revise our notions in time.'

Since 1940, playing with the communal sentiments, the Muslim League could guarantee a rich dividend in the years to come. During the elections held in 1937 for the provincial legislative assemblies, the Muslim League won only 109 out of 492 reserved Muslim seats securing barely 4.8% of the total Muslim votes. In the subsequent elections held in the winter of 1945-46 for the central and provincial legislative assemblies, the League, however, sought the mandate with a straight forward communal slogan—'A vote for the League and Pakistan is a vote for Islam.' Needless to say, the League made a clean sweep of the Muslim seats in the polls casting 76% of the total Muslim votes in India (from 4.8% in 1937).

After the outbreak of the Second World War in September 1939, the Muslim League was assiduously fostered by the then Viceroy Linlithgow and the claim for a separate Muslim state of Pakistan was cleverly used to counter the Congress demand for transfer of actual control of government to the Indians immediately.

After the elections in 1945-46, the League celebrated 11 January 1946, as the Day of Victory and declared that the election results were enough to prove that Muslim League, under the leadership of Mohammad Ali Jinnah, the *Quaid-i-Azam* (great leader), was the sole authority to determine the fate of the Muslims of the region.

Direct Action

On 27 July 1946, the Muslim League Council met at Bombay and Jinnah in his opening speech repeated the demand for Pakistan as the only course left open to the Muslim League. After three days' discussion, the Council passed a resolution rejecting the Cabinet Mission Plan and resorting to 'Direct Action' for achieving Pakistan.

'No power on earth can prevent Pakistan; we shall have India divided or we shall have India destroyed,' Jinnah thundered.

Thus was conceived, in the dark labyrinths 'Direct Action Day' to be observed on 16 August 1946. Endorsing the 'Direct Action', Hajji Sir Khawaja Nazimuddin, who after the early death of Jinnah later became the second

Governor General of Pakistan, threatened,

> 'There are 101 ways in which we can create difficulties, especially when we are not restricted to non-violence. The Moslem population of Bengal knows very well what direct action would mean, and so we need not bother to give them any lead.'[1]

Sir Feroz Khan Noon, who subsequently became the seventh Prime Minister of Pakistan, addressing the Muslim League Legislators' Convention earlier in April 1946, had declared that in the event of their fight,

> 'the havoc which the Muslims would play would put to shame what Chengis Khan and Haiku did.'[2]

In an atmosphere thick with high-pitched communal sentiments, the Communist Party's General Secretary, P C Joshi said after his meeting with the Cabinet Mission that they should,

> 'redraw the boundaries on the basis of natural, ancient homelands of every people, so that re-demarcated provinces became as far as possible linguistically and culturally homogeneous national units, for example, Sind, Pathanland, Western Punjab. The people of each unit should have the unfettered right of self-determination ... the right to decide freely whether they would join the Indian Union or form a separate sovereign state or another Indian Union.'

This led to further uncertainties.[3]

Well before 16 August 1946, a great deal of anxiety prevailed particularly in the province of Bengal, a state geographically located on the eastern part of the Indian dominion, which after the elections of 1946 was under the Government of the Muslim League, with H S Suhrawardy as the Chief Minister. Suhrawardy's inflammable article, under the nom-de-plume of 'Shaheed', published on 5 August 1946 in *The Statesman,* Calcutta, ominously turned out,

> 'Bloodshed and disorder are not necessarily evil in themselves if resorted to for the noble cause. Among Moslems today, no cause is dear or nobler than Pakistan.'

Given the possible Congress protests, a seemingly nervous Bengal Government's declaring 16 August 1946 and the following two consecutive days i.e. 17 and 18 August 1946 as holidays resented the Hindus in particular; the Congress staged a walk out in the Legislative Assembly on 13 August 1946, and confusion reached a new height when the Communist Party of India extended their unconditional support and a series of joint picketing organised by their Comrade Jnan Chakravarty (then Secretary of the Dacca district branch) with the Muslim League to make the 'Direct Action Day' successful.[4]

On the Direct Action Day, also known as the Great Calcutta Riot, the city of Calcutta which was the capital of Bengal, witnessed widespread riot and manslaughter —the day was also marked as the start of what was known as 'The Week of the Long Knives'. Organised bands of armed Muslims were seen moving around the streets rendering the silence of the night with their militant cries and slogans. A huge procession of Muslims, armed with *lathis*, spears and daggers, started from Howrah, the neighbouring city, for Calcutta to attend the mass rally to be presided over by Suhrawardy. After the rally, small Muslim groups seeking easy targets in the unwary vulnerable victims soon transformed into unruly mobs looting the shops of the Hindus as well as nationalist Muslims who did not join the agitation. Private cars were burnt, stray pedestrians were assaulted and stabbed. Only vehicles visible on the streets were the Muslim League lorries and jeeps loaded with hooligans inciting the mob to violence. It was indeed tragic that while the hoodlums were unleashing an unrestrained orgy of murder, arson, rape and looting, the police passively stood by. When the savagery reached its height, Suhrawardy had called for military intervention, which, when it came, was not adequate enough to contain the animosity already rooted in the rival communities.

A British correspondent, Kim Christian, wrote in *The Statesman*, Calcutta,

'I have a stomach made strong by the war experience, but war was never like this. This is not a riot. It needs a word found in the medieval history, a fury. Yet, 'fury' sounds spontaneous and there must have been some deliberation and organisation to see this fury on the way. The hordes who ran about battering and killing with eight-foot *lathis* may have found them lying about or bought them out of their own pockets, but that is hard to believe. We have already commented on the hands who found it easy to get petrol and vehicles when no others were permitted on the streets. It is not mere supposition that men were imported into Calcutta to help in making an impression.'

The protest triggered massive carnage in Calcutta, and within 72 hours more than 5,000 people lost their lives and 100,000 residents in the city were left homeless.

In Bengal, education, trade and industry had almost collapsed owing to recurrent riots. In an unprecedented move, the Bengali intelligentsia communicated to Sir Stafford Cripps and Sir John Anderson that they would strongly support the immediate formation of a separate West Bengal Province guaranteeing under a non-communal ministry, safety of life and unhindered progress in education, industry and commerce, with a continuance and development of Calcutta, a vital part of West Bengal, as a moral, intellectual, social and economic centre. Sir Jadunath Sarkar, Dr Meghnad Saha, Dr Sisir Mitra, Prof Suniti Kumar Chatterjee were the most prominent exponents among the signatories. Almost simultaneously, 10,000 telegrams were also sent to the Viceroy urging the Partition of Bengal.[5]

Syama Prasad Mookerjee, the *Godfather* of the modern *Hindutva*, founded the Bharatiya Jana Sangh which was considered to be the first Hindu nationalist political party of its kind. Mookerjee was also the leader of the Hindu Mahasabha and closely associated with the RSS. Initially a stiff opponent to the Partition, following the fratricidal brutality in 'Great Calcutta Riot' orchestrated by Suhrawardy, Mookerjee strongly advocated against the Hindus living in a Muslim-dominated state government controlled by the Muslim League. A staunch opponent to the Partition was thus transformed into the ardent advocate of the Partition of Bengal.

Communal fury widens

In Calcutta, the violence was fast becoming a firestorm large enough to set the whole country ablaze, especially in Bengal and Punjab with the Muslim League continuing its inflammatory propaganda depicting the 'Hindus as enemies' and proclaiming its resolve to take Pakistan by force. Disturbing reports of unrest and lawlessness poured in from all over. 'Life and property are unsafe in eastern Bengal,' wrote one correspondent in *The Statesman,* dated 30 September 1946. 'Gangsters operate on railway lines, stop trains at places of their choice, rob and carry away the booty by boats or bullock carts before the news reaches the next station.'

In Noakhali, a district situated in south-eastern Bengal, the first outburst took place where Hindus suffered a pogrom and were almost annihilated. Murder, rape and forcible conversion of the Hindus, the minority in the district, took place on a scale unprecedented in the history. Muriel Lester reporting in the *Hindustan Standard,* dated 8 November 1946 wrote,

'The worst of all was the plight of the women. Several of them had to watch their husbands being murdered and then were forcibly converted to Islam and married to those responsible for their death. These women had a dead look. It was not despair, nothing so active as that. It was utter blankness ... The eating of beef and declaration of allegiance to Islam has been forced upon many thousands as the price of their lives ...Perhaps the only thing that can be quite positively asserted about this orgy of arson and violence is that it was not a spontaneous uprising of the villagers. Howsoever many *goondas* may live in Bengal, they are incapable of organising this campaign on their own initiative. Houses have been sprayed with petrol and burnt. Who supplied the rationed fuel? Who imported stirrup-pumps into this rural areas? Who supplied the weapons? . . . The *goondas* seem to think that they really are the rulers of this beautiful area of Bengal. One sees no sign of fear among those who had stood by and watched destruction, tyranny and aggression; anxiety as to further punishment does not seem to exist.'

On hearing the harrowing tales of genocide in Noakhali, Gandhiji decided to tour that area with a view to restore peace. He left for Noakhali on 6 November 1946 with his peace mission and visited a large number of villages during his sojourn. Explaining his mission, in one of his letters, Gandhi said,

'My present mission is the most complicated and difficult one of my life. I can sing (with Cardinal Newman) with cent per cent truth: *The night is dark and I am far from home. Lead Thou me on.* I never experienced such darkness in my life before. The night seems long. The only consolation is that I feel neither baffled nor disappointed. I am prepared for any eventuality. "Do or Die" has to be put to test here. "Do" here means Hindus and Muslims should learn to live together in peace and amity. Otherwise,

I should die in the attempt. It is really a difficult test. God's will be done.'[6]

From Calcutta and Noakhali, rioting spread over to the neighbouring province of Bihar particularly in the form of reprisals where the majority Hindus came down heavily on the minorities. Gandhiji wrote to Pandit Nehru,

> 'The news from Bihar has shaken me. My inner voice tells me: you may not live to be a witness to this senseless slaughter. If people refuse to see what is clear as daylight and pay no heed to what you say, does it not mean that your day is over. The logic of the argument is driving me irresistibly towards a fast. I, therefore, propose to issue a statement that unless this orgy of madness ceases, I must go on fast unto death . . .'[7]

As a consequence of the 'Great Calcutta Killing', the Noakhali tragedy, and the Bihar frenzy, Gandhiji's dream of an undivided India was completely shattered.

~

Transfer of Power

With a view to organising the transfer of power, amidst the communal turbulence, Lord Wavell called upon both the Congress and the League functionaries to join the Viceroy's Executive Council. Jinnah citing the hesitant and conditional approval of the Congress to the Cabinet Mission Plan rescinded League approval and declined to join any Interim Coalition Government. Congress accepted the offer, and on 2 September 1946, Pandit Jawaharlal Nehru assumed office as Vice President, Viceroy's Executive Council, *de facto* the Prime Minister of India with Sardar Vallabhbhai Patel having the charge of Home Affairs.

Jinnah proclaimed this day as the day of mourning and a black flag demonstration was staged by the Muslim League before the Secretariat at New Delhi, and disturbances took place throughout the country. The Muslim League declined a subsequent offer from Pandit Nehru to join the Council and felt let down by the British authorities, with the disappointment manifested in fierce agitation all over the country.

Lord Wavell, in the greater interest of restoring communal harmony, once again invited Jinnah; after a series of meetings with the Viceroy, on 25 October 1946, the Muslim League reversed their decision to take part in the coalition administration. Sarat Chandra Bose, Sir Safat Ahmed Khan and Syed Ali Zaheer from the Congress party decided to step down from the cabinet berths in order to accommodate their Muslim League colleagues. Lord Wavell's recommendation was to offer at least an important portfolio to the League, and his personal suggestion was the Home Affairs for a League member.

Sardar Vallabhbhai Patel vehemently opposed the idea of handing over the Home portfolio to a Muslim League member; after a great deal of deliberation within the inner circle, the Congress party offered the Finance portfolio to the League and Liyaqat Ali stepped in. Incidentally, Liyaqat Ali later became the first Prime Minister of Pakistan. Since the Interim Government was born in the midst of suspicion and mistrust between the Congress and the Muslim League, the Council functioning was often marked by internal frictions and thwarting of decisions which often led to impasse.

As Finance chief, Liaqat Ali was prone to intervene in each and every issue resulting in complete administrative deadlock. Sardar Patel, who had been happy to retain his Home portfolio in exchange for finance, realised bitterly that all the departmental proposals would be subject to Liaqat Ali's approval or modification—a situation which made it almost impossible for any Congress member in the Council to discharge services in any effective manner. Internal discord thus escalated.

᠙

Mountbatten replaces Wavell . . . Partition hastened

After the Calcutta, Noakhali and Bihar disasters, communal tension was intensifying. Reports of skirmishes between communities all over the country became the order of the day, and the whole situation was so volatile that a major showdown was likely. Lord Wavell knew that he had to restore peace among the dissenting communal factions before a complete transfer of power could proceed. Although the date of 30 June 1948 was fixed as the deadline for the transfer of power to the Indians, Lord Wavell wanted to postpone the process until peace was brought back, because in his opinion, a withdrawal of British forces would lead to widespread rioting and disturbances with Indian political leaders unable to control the situation. Lord Wavell realised that,

'history would never pardon if the British legacy, having ruled the country for over hundred years, left the ground in the lurch.'

Clement Attlee, on the other hand, did not want to wait. Lord Wavell thus resigned and Lord Mountbatten replaced him on 24 March 1947 as Viceroy in India.

Meanwhile, the situation was fast deteriorating, particularly in the west. So far Punjab had shown restraint but events had taken a different direction since the Akali Dal viewed the Cabinet Mission's proposals were distressing because the proposed grouping of States was putting the Sikhs under a Muslim majority. Although in a conciliation process, a collection of Sikh political parties had joined the Interim Coalition Government headed by Jawaharlal Nehru, any rapprochement from the Muslim League proved elusive, and Muslim–Sikh riots erupted.

One of the co-founders of the of Vishwa Hindu Parishad and then undisputed political and religious leader of the Sikh community, Master Tara Singh's protest in Lahore on 3 March 1947 proclaiming 'Death to Pakistan' ignited the volatile situation. In early March 1947, thus Lahore witnessed a bloody communal battle killing thirteen and leaving hundreds seriously injured. The bloodbath continued with the Sikhs being made the special targets of the Muslim rioters. Nehru flew over to the riot affected areas, and in Rawalpindi he was shown the deep well into which Sikh and Hindu women had jumped to save their honour. In a milieu of impending civil war, the Akali Dal agreed, as a matter of principle, to the Partition of India.

In Sind, the atmosphere was charged with communal hatred and mistrust leading to a large fall out.

> 'It was Jinnah and the Moslem riots and massacres, that convinced me of two things soon after my arrival' as Lord Mountbatten, the new Viceroy in India recalled to Richard Hough, his biographer.

> 'Jinnah was the Moslem League. He held the future of India in his hand . . . but it was almost impossible to warm him. He had only one dream, and that was a separate Moslem state. Jinnah was cold, arrogant, vain, inflexible—all the characteristics that made negotiation virtually impossible.'[8]

Lord Mountbatten seized the earliest opportunity of taking control of the administration and he started impressing on both the Congress and the Muslim League leaders that division of Indian territory to create Pakistan was the only plausible alternative. Jinnah once more put forth his proposal for exchanging populations 'to avoid the recurrence of incidents which had taken place where small minorities have been butchered by overwhelming majorities.'

Gandhiji was dead against the Partition of India. He said,

> 'I can never be a willing party to the vivisection. I would employ non-violent means to prevent it . . .

My whole soul rebels against the idea that Hinduism and Islam represent two antagonistic cultures and doctrines. To assent to such a doctrine is for me denial of God.'

With all the strength at his command, he declared:

'If the Congress wishes to accept Partition, it will be over my dead body. So long as I am alive, I will never agree to the Partition of India. Nor will I, if I can help it, allow the Congress to accept it.'

Gandhiji was prepared to accept the demand of the Muslim League as put forth in the Lahore resolution, namely, self-determination for the areas where the Muslims were in majority, but he was of the opinion that self-determination could not be exercised in the absence of freedom. Gandhiji added that India should first agree to unite to achieve Independence.

According to Jinnah, the Muslims formed a separate nation by virtue of their *distinctive culture and civilisation, language and literature, art and architecture, names and nomenclature, sense of value and proportion, legal laws and moral codes, customs and calendars, history and tradition,* and therefore, he argued, 'they were entitled to a separate, sovereign existence in a homeland of their own.' The talks could not be prolonged further. Addressing the audience, after one of his prayer-meetings, Gandhiji said,

I have tried my level best to go as far as I could, to meet the Quaid-I-Azam's viewpoint. I have taken incalculable pains to understand him and to make myself understood, but I have failed.

Gandhiji himself described in one of the meetings saying, 'He (Jinnah) wants Pakistan now, not after Independence. "We will have Independence for Pakistan and Hindustan", he said. "We should come to an agreement and then go to the Government and ask them to accept it, force them to accept our solution!" I (Gandhi) said, I could never ask the Britishers to impose partition on India. If you all want to separate, I can't stop you. I have not got the power to compel you and I would not use it, if I had'. Gandhiji asserted, "The Muslims want Pakistan, the League represents Muslims and it wants Pakistan".'

Gandhi being marginalised

Contrary to the wish of Gandhiji, the Congress leaders were ready to accept Partition in return for an early transfer of power to escape the intrigues of the British officials and continued obstruction by the Muslim League in the Interim Government. With injured vanity, Patel, who had swallowed the bitter pill of the Muslim League in the Interim Coalition Council, was convinced that it was next to impossible to work in any manner with the League, and thus when Lord Mountbatten had mooted the idea of Partition offering solution to the present impasse, Patel gracefully nodded as he became certain that Hindus and Muslims could not be united in one nation. Ultimately, the Congress Working Committee (CWC) acceded to Partition. Gandhiji was not consulted in the historic decision and he was further disillusioned when Nehru clarified that 'now a time for decision has come and merely passing of resolutions giving expression to our views meant little. I felt convinced and so did most of the members of the Working Committee that we must press for immediate division so that reality might be brought into (the) picture.'

Justifying the decision of the CWC, Sardar Vallabhbhai Patel declared,

> 'The Working Committee has not acted out of fear. But I am afraid of one thing, that all our toil and hard work of these many years might go waste or prove unfruitful . . . Except for a few honourable exceptions, Muslim officials from the top down to the chaprasis are working for the League. . . . Whether we like it or not, *de facto* Pakistan already exists in Punjab and Bengal. Under the circumstances, I would prefer a *de jure* Pakistan, which may make the League more responsible. Freedom is coming. We have 75 to 80 per cent of India, which we can make strong with our own genius. The League can develop the rest of the country.'[9]

Patel's thesis almost echoed the Hindu nationalist political philosophy, propagated by Savarkar's declaration in 1937 at the Hindu Mahasabha session, popularly known as *Hindu Rashtra Darshan* at Karnavati (Ahemdabad) that

> 'the Mohammedans are likely to prove dangerous to our Hindu nation. India cannot be assumed today to be a unitarian and homogeneous nation. On the contrary, there are two nations in the main, the Hindus and the Muslims in India.'

In 1938, at the Nagpur Session, Savarkar being the second term elected president of the Hindu Mahasabha, went one step further rejecting the concept of Indian nationalism on which the entire freedom movement led by the Congress was based,

'The original political sin, which our Hindu Congressites . . . committed at the beginning of the Indian National Congress movement and are persistently committing still on running after the mirage of a territorial Indian Nation and of seeking to kill as an impediment in that fruitless pursuit the life growth of an organic Hindu Nation. . . . We Hindus are a Nation by ourselves because religious, racial, cultural and historical affinities bind us intimately into a homogenous nation.'

This is the concept of 'cultural nationalism' as opposed to 'territorial nationalism'. Everyone born in India does not belong to 'the nation'. He must also accept the credo of Hindutva, 'cultural nationalism'. As Savarkar put it,

'The Hindus are the nation in India—in Hindusthan, and the Moslem a minority community.'

 festoon

Gandhi's last attempt to thwart Partition

Criticising the genesis of the issue that forced the Partition, Maulana Abul Kalam Azad, the follower of

Hindu-Muslim harmony in the Congress party, did not, however, endorse the arguments of Patel while stating,
'It would not perhaps be unfair to say that Vallabhbhai Patel was the founder of Indian partition.'[10]

Communal riots by then stretched beyond Punjab and other areas too. Lord Mountbatten, in an urgent message, called upon Gandhi and other Indian leaders including Jinnah for discussions. Abandoning his peace mission in Bihar, Gandhiji had to leave Patna (Bihar) on 30 March 1947 to attend the political conference at Delhi.

India's partition, the most contentious happening in the history of the twentieth century after the Second World War, divided the leaders in accordance with their political convictions. In the words of Pandit Nehru,

'They had cut off their head to get rid of their headaches. They got relief no more than an amputee, who is left with his "phantom limb", aching worse than ever, even after the affected member has been removed.'

On the other hand, Jinnah was jubilant, and he congratulated the Muslims of non-Pakistan areas for their labour and sacrifices that helped in the realisation of Pakistan. Not fully satisfied with the securing of Pakistan, the Muslim League now adopted the slogans,

'Hans ke liya hai Pakistan, larke lenge Hindustan' (We have achieved Pakistan in fun, we shall now take Hindustan by force).

In order to thwart the impending partition, Gandhiji had made a last moment appeal that the Congress would invite Jinnah to form the Interim Government and choose his own Cabinet which, Bapu was certain, would win over the Muslim League and the country would be saved from being divided on communal basis. Initially, Lord Mountbatten was impressed by this idea, but by that time Gandhiji had become yesterday's man for the Congress, and the stalwarts in the party simply forced Bapu to withdraw the proposal. In the process, Gandhiji was branded as a spokesman of the Muslims, yet again.

On this occasion, Gandhiji wrote a letter to the Viceroy, Lord Mountbatten, who agreed that the formation of Pakistan was undesirable but simultaneously felt that the Congress High Command were 'now quite anxious for it to happen as soon as possible'. Gandhiji observed with a heavy heart that his place was in Bihar and Noakhali rather than in Delhi.

On 3 June 1947, following the resolution adopted in the CWC, the ultimate decision to divide India was broadcast over All India Radio. First came the official announcement, followed by broadcast statements from Mountbatten, Nehru, Jinnah and Baldev Singh. A feeling of disappointment, frustration, anger and gloom throughout the country was looming large; enthusiasm for the long awaited 15 August 1947, the day of independence, was absent. Gandhiji declared: 'It must be a day for prayer and soul-searching.' He hoped against hope that 'there is one condition on which it might become a day for universal rejoicing in spite of the decision. Let Hindus and Muslims both try from now to become true friends, so that they are ready on 15 August to give themselves to rejoicing.' Freedom had come but it left the Mahatma cold, 'At last, after two hundred years, Britain had conquered India!' He moaned.

❦

15 August 1947, India's Independence Day

Amidst glittering lights and loud slogans awaiting the dawn of freedom, Pandit Nehru said in a poetic assertion,

'At the stroke of the midnight hour when the world sleeps, India will awake to life and freedom and a soul of a nation long suppressed will find utterance.'

On the other hand, refusing to take part in the nation's Independence carnival at Delhi, Mahatma Gandhi remained in a Muslim–dominated slum in Calcutta, giving a healing touch from his fasting bed to a riot-torn society and appealing to people to maintain peace. In his evening prayer meeting, he said,

'We'll be free tomorrow but the country will split tonight.'

When life was slowly ebbing away from the frail framework of the Mahatma, people from across the society came and pledged for communal harmony. In Calcutta, Hindus and Muslims hoisted India's national flag together while rioting continued unabated in Punjab. Mountbatten later said, 'while the 55,000-man boundary force in Punjab was swamped by riots, the one-man boundary force brought peace to Bengal'.

On 15 August 1947, while Delhi was rejoicing at the birth of an independent state, distressing news of massacres and bloodshed started pouring in from various parts of the country. India's partition and independence brought with it a scourge of violence that swept across the country. The blood of thousands of innocent men and women flowed in the Beas, Chenab, Jhelum, Ravi, and Sutlej, the five rivers of Punjab, and thousands of women were kidnapped and raped in the presence of the Army. Giving a graphic description of the situation in Punjab, Sardar Patel wrote to Gandhiji,

'The people there have simply gone mad. Cities and villages are being burnt down. Men are being cut to pieces like vegetables. Reports are coming in that the military and the police are involved in it. It has become difficult to obtain accurate information as to what is happening in the land of the five rivers. It was a war, the first of its kind, waged by the combatants against non-combatants with whom they had no cause to quarrel, and helpless men, women and children were brutally massacred.'[11]

Communal rage reaches a new height

Subsequent to the official announcement of Partition, communal fury reached a new height. Huge convoys of non-Muslims, each 30,000 to 40,000 strong with their

cattle and bullock-carts, were crossing over to India from
Western-Punjab on foot. Hindu and Sikh refugees were
clambering atop railway carriages—possibly the biggest
movement of population in world history. All modes of
transportation were employed for the purpose of
evacuation. Between 27 August and 6 November 1947,
673 trains were run to ferry over 2,799,000 refugees to
India. Over 427,000 non-Muslims were carried during the
same period by means of approximately 1,200 military
and civil motor vehicles. More than 27,000 evacuees were
brought to India by government chartered planes in 962
flights between 15 September and 7 December 1947. In
addition, a large numbers of the displaced were attacked
while crossing the border to India while outbreaks of
cholera and other epidemics added to their misery,
thousands perishing on the way. On 21 August 1947,
morning newspapers carried news of the slaughter of
Hindu and Sikh refugees from the North–West Frontier
Provinces who were returning to India at Gujaranwala,
a railway station in West Punjab which had become part
of Pakistan.

Grieving at this tragic turn of the events, Gandhiji
addressed a meeting at the All India Congress
Committee. He emphasised,

'I repeat that it is your prime duty to treat Muslims
as your brothers, no matter what happens in
Pakistan . . . Restraint will add to your strength . . .
If, on the other hand, you approve of what has
happened, you must change the very creed and
character of the All India Congress Committee . . .
Let all Muslims who have left their homes and fled
to Pakistan come back here.'

Gandhiji realised, much to his disappointment, that the Congress colleagues were fast losing faith in the lone sentinel of the Hindu-Muslim accord. Expressing his helplessness and anguish, Gandhiji, in one of his prayer meetings mentioned that

'whatever the Congress decides will be done; nothing will be according to what I say. My writ runs no more . . . No one listens to me anymore.'

Gandhiji was often scornfully told to *retire to the Himalayas*. Even Sardar Patel was no longer Gandhiji's 'Yes-Man'. His utterances about the vast majority of the Indian Muslims being against Congress ideals were deeply resented by Mahatma. On numerous occasions, Gandhiji did not endorse Patel's deeds. Millions of Hindus and Sikhs who fled the newly created Pakistan to India took refuge at make-shift camps in Delhi, and Maulana Azad took the responsibility for the safety of Muslims in India, touring affected areas in Bengal, Bihar, Assam and Punjab organising refugee camps, supplies and security. Azad gave speeches to large crowds encouraging peace and calm in the border areas and giving confidence to Muslims across the country to remain in India and not fear for their safety and security. Focusing on bringing the capital of Delhi back to a state of peace, Azad organised security and relief efforts, but was drawn into a dispute with Sardar Patel, the then Deputy Prime Minister (in charge of Home Affairs) over the issue of the removal of Mohinder Singh Randhawa, ICS, the then *de facto* Commissioner of Delhi who was a clean shaven Sikh. Reposing faith in Randhawa, Patel, however, argued that the commissioner was not biased, and if his dismissal was forced, it would provoke anger amongst the Hindus and Sikhs and divide the city police. Patel was also criticised by Nehru, secular Muslims and condemned by Gandhi over his alleged wish to see Muslims from other parts of India depart. While Patel vehemently denied such allegations, the Muslim leaders also criticised him for neglecting the needs of Muslims leaving for Pakistan, and concentrating resources for incoming Hindu and Sikh refugees instead. In Cabinet meetings and discussions with Gandhi, Patel and Azad clashed over security issues in Delhi and Punjab, as well as the allocation of resources for relief and rehabilitation. Patel opposed Azad and Nehru's proposal to reserve the houses vacated by Muslims who had departed for Pakistan for Muslims in India displaced by the violence. Patel argued that a secular government could not offer preferential treatment for any religious community, while Azad remained anxious to assure the rehabilitation of Muslims in India.

Punjab was in flames and the situation in the Sind was also fast deteriorating with disturbances breaking out in Karachi on 6 January 1948. The exodus from Bengal continued and the Congress High Command was unable to prevent it. Gandhiji felt isolated from his colleagues, and could see no peace in the hearts of the people. He wrote,

'Today man fears man, neighbour distrusts neighbour. How strange that the peace of a country that won its independence through *Ahimsa* is deemed to be safe only under the protection of *Himsa*!'

Gandhiji's last fast

Gandhiji, the frail old man of 78 years feeling utterly helpless in the face of the communal hatred started his 'fast unto death' on 13 January 1948 at the Birla House, Delhi so the country would not witness vultures feasting on the fratricidal dead bodies anymore.

While thousands of people across the religious faith showed solidarity behind the fasting *Satyagrahi* on the eve of 15 August 1947 at Calcutta, rage was sweeping the country at the conditions Gandhiji had set for ending his fast. A fast by Bapu, perhaps for the first time, caused nationwide resentment. There was a feeling of utter frustration among the displaced people languishing in refugee transit camps supported by the limited government assistance amidst utter chaos. A section of the Indian people, particularly the refugees from the Punjab and the followers of the Hindu Mahasabha, the Hindu nationalist outfit as well as the Rashtriya Swayamsevak Sangh, another extremist Hindu organisation, had been critical of Gandhiji's views right from the beginning. Congress under Gandhi's leadership committed one blunder after another, which gave an upper hand to Mohammad Ali Jinnah and ultimately the Congress was obliged to accept Pakistan. When in early September 1944, after his release from prison in May 1944, Gandhiji approached Jinnah for a political solution and came back empty handed after having spent 18 days with Jinnah at his Bombay residence, it gave a new and added importance to Jinnah who was almost in political oblivion once he had left the Congress in the twenties.

Delhi, the capital of the newly independent India, was most affected by the growing refugee population, and the situation was worsening with every moment. In order to escape from the biting cold and misery, many took shelter in the desolate mosques and other Muslim properties available in Delhi, blaming the Muslims for their precarious condition. Dr Zakir Hussain, who later became the President of India, described that the ill-fated refugees as being buried in 'living graves'.

Adding to the ill-feeling was Mahatma's advice to vacate the mosques and other Muslim properties and return to their respective liability camps. Gandhiji's view that 'the life of even a puny Moslem in this country must be protected' also aggravated the turmoil while his commitment to giving 550 million rupees to Pakistan as a major condition of breaking his fast exasperated the general population and divided the government.

On 13 January 1948, Jayaprakash Narayan, popularly known as JP, an ardent disciple of Mahatma Gandhi and a renowned social reform leader came to Bombay to deliver a speech at St Xavier's College Auditorium. JP warned,

'Delhi is in turmoil today. Even Maulana Abul Kalam Azad is not free to move around there . . . In order to annihilate communalism, Mahatmaji is risking his life . . .'

Besides the arch-rival RSS, the refugees, especially the Hindu and Sikh displaced migrants in the west started openly being abusive about Gandhiji and Congress party over the Partition and the subsequent ordeal they had been subjected to. They nicknamed Gandhiji, *Mohammad Gandhi*', '*Jinnah's slave*' and protested against his recital of verses from the Koran. Disturbances were caused at his prayer-meetings also. Even pamphlets were distributed threatening Gandhiji's life and the Sikhs carried black banners shouting 'Blood for Blood', 'We want revenge', and 'Let Gandhi die!'

Despite the fury, on 18 January 1948, after the Reserve Bank of India had transferred 450 million rupees to Pakistan and the All Party Peace Committee had given an assurance in writing, signed by the Hindu Mahasabha in Delhi and the RSS, assuring the maintenance of peace, law and order, Gandhiji accepted a glass of orange juice from Maulana Azad and terminated his fast at 12.45 pm.[12]

On the same day, after the end of Mahatma's five day long fast, Pandit Nehru was addressing a large gathering at Subzi Mandi, an area in Delhi predominantly inhabited by the Muslim community. A Sikh refugee group was passing by in which Madanlal was the key activist, and they shouted anti-Pakistan slogans and in the mayhem Madanlal dared touch Nehru's daughter Indira's hand. Nehru was furious but Madanlal told him,

'You are disturbed because I only touched your daughter's hand—what about us who have seen our mothers, sisters and daughters raped before our eyes?'

Madanlal was arrested and released after being branded as yet another disgruntled refugee, only to be re-arrested two days later for a much more serious crime.

౿౨

Madanlal tells me all

After his release in October 1964, Madanlal paid a visit to my Shivaji Park house just before his marriage. Madanlal reconstructed the whole incident of his abortive attack on Bapu on 20 January 1948. I came to know lot more than I had gathered as the Chief Prosecution Witness in the Murder Trial.

On 13 January 1948, Nathrum Godse and Narayan Apte, the proprietor of *Hindu Rashtra*, the Marathi daily, were at their office at Poona, a city in Maharashtra about 60 miles away from Bombay situated on the Deccan plateau. While the duo was busy screening the teleprinter dispatches, suddenly a news flash caught their attention.

Despite earnest requests from different communities, Gandhiji had turned down entreaties to call off the fast. What left the Poona Brahmins aghast was Gandhi's insistence that Hindu and Sikh refugees should be sent back to Pakistan, and Muslims who had left India should be brought back. Gandhi's insistence on paying the 550 million rupees to Pakistan, they were convinced, would be utilised by the League Government in Pakistan to grab Jammu & Kashmir from India. The decision was instant—Gandhi had to go.

At a secluded corner of the Hindu Rashtra office, it was on the same day, 13 January 1948, Godse, Apte, Madanlal, and Madanlal's 'seth' Vishnu Karkare, a Hindu Mahasabhite and Deccan Guest House owner at Ahmednagar, solemnly took the pledge to kill Gandhiji.

All they required were arms and ammunition. It was around 8.30 pm in the dark winter evening when Apte, Karkare, Madanlal, Om Prakash, and Chopra had met at a ramshackle tea-stall on their way to 'Shastra Bhandar', a storehouse of weapons, owned by Digambar Badge, disguised as a 'Sadhu'.

In November 1947, while Narayan Apte was proceeding to Bhor, he met Digambar Badge, another Hindutva scion. It was a sheer coincidence. Badge shared a similar political ideology and was, indeed, a God-sent associate whom Apte wanted to utilise for his *great mission*. After their pilgrimage at Bhor, both the perpetrators had come back to Poona to attend a long series of clandestine meetings and surreptitious conferences with a handful of figures whom the history of Indian politics should remember only as dark figures.

Badge welcomed his comrades, and calmly called out to his servant Shankar for the 'stuff', and it was promptly brought out from the place where it was securely kept by Badge's trusted confidant Shankar. In fact, the 'stuff' was a collection of arms consisting of gun-cotton slabs, hand-grenades, cartridges, pistols, and fuse wires. The only thing which was bothering Apte was the absence of a revolver which, despite several attempts, Badge could not procure for the *great mission*.

On 13 January 1948, Nathuram V Godse effected the nominations on his two life policies; one in favour of the wife of Narayan Apte, and the other one, in favour of the wife of his brother, Gopal Godse while Narayan Apte remained witness to both the nominations. At about the same time, Gopal Godse applied for seven days' leave to his employer starting from 15 January 1948.

On the very next day Nathuram Godse and Apte left for Bombay. Badge and Shankar had already reached Bombay with their consignment to be handed over to the duo. It was also the day when Nathuram Godse paid Gopal, his brother, Rs 250 to arrange for a revolver—

for Badge had given in—through his contacts at Poona Military Store in which Gopal was working for a long time. It was the same day when in the evening Nathuram and Narayan being accompanied by Digambar were looking for an opportune moment to sneak into a bungalow at Keluskar Road, Bombay; 'Savarkar Sadan' was the name inscribed on the bungalow gate. Digambar was kept outside the gate possibly to keep a watch while Nathuram and Narayan went in with the 'stuff' carrying in a bag they had collected from Digambar. After a lapse of five to ten minutes, the duo came back carrying the same bag with them. The Brahmins from Poona were cheerful as Savarkar had decided that Mahatma Gandhi, Pandit Jawaharlal Nehru and Suhrawardy *should be finished off* and entrusted such a dire task on Nathuram Godse, Narayan Apte and the rest.

Hindu Mahasabha Bhawan at Dadar was the next destination. Shankar did once again join the team to visit Dixit Maharaj, the spiritual leader of the affluent Hindu sect, Pushtimarg Vaishanavas, at his house at Bhuleshwar where the bag containing the 'stuff' was left behind. Madanlal emerged at the Hindu Mahasabha Bhawan and in their nocturnal rendezvous Madanlal had been informed about how far their plan had proceeded.

On the morning of 15 January 1948, Narayan Apte booked two air tickets from Bombay under assumed names for the afternoon flight leaving for Delhi on 17 January 1948. At all the crucial junctions, as C K Daphtary, Advocate General of Bombay, who appeared as Chief Public Prosecutor in the trial case would point out later, the 'assumed names' and separate means of travelling were only to avoid the risk of leaving clues to their real identities and cruel design.

On the same day, Apte and Nathuram Godse had a brief discussion on their proceedings with Badge, Shankar, and Madanlal at the Hindu Mahasabha Bhawan, and thereafter Shankar, Badge, Nathuram, and Apte went to a place called the Agrani Printing Press to meet its owner G M Joshi. In the midst of their conference, Karkare appeared and joined them. Shankar had, however, remained outside.

At the end of the meeting everyone, except Joshi, went back to the Hindu Mahasabha Bhawan wherefrom Apte, Nathuram, Karkare, Madanlal, and Badge went to Dixit Maharaj's house to get back the bag containing the 'stuff'. In a brief discussion, Apte decided on the spot where Karkare and Madanlal should keep the 'stuff' and leave for Delhi immediately that night itself.

Apte then asked Dixit Maharaj if he could procure a revolver or two for him. Maharaj was not certain but he did certainly comfort him that he would try to get some for them all. On coming out from Dixit Maharaj's house, Apte asked Badge if he was mentally prepared to follow them in their dangerous errand any further. Badge agreed to be a part of their *noble* mission.

Both Karkare and Madanlal that night boarded the last available train which would take them to Delhi on 17 January 1948 where they were to meet Godse and Apte who were reaching there by Air India flight DC3. Karkare and Madanlal reached Delhi early in the morning of 17 January 1948 and decided to check in at Sharif Hindu Hotel under assumed names.

On 16 January 1948, Badge and Shankar returned to Poona to join Nathuram Godse who was already there to meet his brother Gopal Godse before the *glorious act*. In their meeting, Nathuram Godse asked Badge to join him at Bombay. Soon Badge and Shankar left for Bombay. On their way, Shankar got out at Dadar heading for Hindu Mahasabha Bhawan while Badge reached Bombay where Nathuram Godse and Narayan Apte were already present. A taxi was engaged for their desperate move to pull funds, and the duo, along with Badge, at first, went to the Bombay Dyeing Mills where they had met Charandas Meghji Mathur Das, and collected a sum of Rs 1,000 from him. Having been successful in procuring some funds, they then returned to Hindu Mahasabha Bhawan where Shankar was waiting for them.

All the while something was going on in Nathuram Godse's mind which prompted him to propose that they should have the last *darshan* (sight) of their mentor, Savarkar. So they all had proceeded to Savarkar's house in the same taxi. With the exception of Shankar who was left in the taxi, every one of them walked into the house. Badge was asked to wait on the first floor for them to come back, while Nathuram Godse and Narayan Apte proceeded to meet Savarkar.

As they came out of Savarkar's room, after a brief discussion, the Hindutva commander was heard to cry out to the duo, *'Yashasvi Houn Ya'* (be successful and come). Such was the bold farewell remark that it impregnated Godse with improbity, with a mantle of seeming glory and patriotism that kept reverberating in Godse's heart. He was the chosen one to do a great and noble deed for India; he the hand, while Savarkar the contriving intelligence. Savarkar's aim was made obvious at that meeting. Even in the presence of the taxi-driver (later to be identified as Itapa Kotian) Savarkar, while seeing them off, had remarked,

'Gandhiji's 100 years are over!'

In the next turn, the comrades collected more than Rs 1,000 rupees from Afzalpurkar, Kale, and Patankar, and headed for Dixit Maharaj. Although promised earlier, Maharaj could not yet procure one revolver for the *great mission*. Apte was always prompt in taking spontaneous decisions; Apte gave Rs 350 to Badge and asked him to proceed to Delhi on his own by train.

The next destination for the Poona Brahmins was Santa Cruz Airport, Bombay.

On arriving at Delhi, Nathuram Godse and Narayan Apte had stayed at Marina Hotel as 'S Deshpande' and 'M Deshpande'. Subsequently, on 19 January 1948, Badge and Shankar had arrived at Delhi, and straightway they had gone to the Hindu Mahasabha Bhawan where they had put up in a room in which Madanlal and Gopal were already staying. Soon Nathuram Godse, Apte, and Karkare came to have a dialogue with their colleagues.

Next day, 20 January 1948, turned out to be a very hectic day for Narayan Apte and his accomplices; tension was mounting up right from the morning. A few calculations were required as regards their vicious operation of killing Mahatma Gandhi; calculations and measurements were supposed to have been done perfectly so that every step of the operation went smoothly and without courting danger unto themselves. In the morning, they went to the Hindu Mahasabha Bhawan, and there Apte had asked Badge and Shankar to follow him to the Birla House. As they tried to get down at the main entrance of the Birla House, they were promptly intercepted by the *chowkidar*. However, they made attempts to convince the *chowkidar* that all they wanted was to see the Secretary to Mahatmaji; and thereafter they held out a small note introducing themselves, albeit falsely, and stating their business with him. The *chowkidar* took the chit and went inside for the secretary. On having seen a man coming out from the Birla House, Apte pointed out to Badge stating that the man was Suhrawardy, another 'target' of Savarkar who would be finished off after Gandhi. While the front portals were being left unattended by any guard, the cunning trio quickly got into the premises without tarrying and made their way to the ground. Apte pointed out to Badge the place where Mahatma Gandhi used to hold his prayers, and they soon started taking measurements of the openings of a window with trellis-work. Apte told Badge that through that opening a revolver shot could be fired and they could, with a little care, throw a hand-grenade from the room behind. Apte also showed the place where a gun-cotton slab was to be exploded to divert the attention of the people who would have assembled at the prayer-ground. It was the other most important part of the operation because to reach the core of the hive, one would need to disperse the swarms of bees that mantle it so thickly.

Another most important task to perform was to try the pistol. So on returning to the Hindu Mahasabha Bhawan, Apte suggested to Gopal that he should accompany him to the jungle behind the Hindu Mahasabha Bhawan and try the pistol there. Badge and Shankar soon joined them and having tested the pistol they all returned to the Bhawan after sometime. Later on, Apte, Karkare, Madanlal, Badge, Shankar, and Gopal Godse went to Room no 40 of the Marina Hotel. At that time Nathuram Godse was alone, reclined in bed.

After the arms and ammunition were distributed among them all, Nathuram Godse warned Badge that it was their last attempt and the work should be accomplished successfully. As soon as Madanlal had ignited the gun-cotton slab and the assembled people started dispersing, the others could shoot Gandhiji. Nathuram Godse and Apte were to give signals to Badge and Madanlal respectively.

Madanlal's attack on Mahatma

Two on-the-spot inspections were carried away, successfully, and specific tasks were assigned to the individual members. Yet Madanlal, the chief commander, was sweating in Room no 40 of Marina Hotel in the chilling cold of Delhi's winter. By 4.30 pm, everyone viz. Madanlal Kishanlal Pahwa, Nathuram Vinayak Godse, Narayan Dattatreya Apte, Vishnu Ramkrishna Karkare, Digambar Ramchandra Badge, Gopal Godse and Shankar Kistaiya congregated at the Birla House. Madanlal and Karkare were the first two to reach Birla House by *tonga* while others reached the prayer meeting one after the other ferried by a green Chevrolet cab PBF 671; Nathuram was the last man to enter the scene.

It was just two days after breaking his fast, in the prayer meeting, Mahatma was expressing his distress over the on-going communal turmoil across the geographical borders. Visibly weakened, Bapu's voice was so feeble that Sushila Nayar volunteered to play the role of an interpreter.

All the gang members disguised as devotees to the great soul, Mahatma, were in position. As Godse and Apte had meticulously planned, Madanlal would plant a bomb near to the podium where Gandhiji would be addressing his disciples. As soon as the blast would take place, causing a pandemonium, Badge would open fire at Bapu almost from a point blank range while Gopal would explode another grenade ensuring that panic sustained. After the attack, all the gang members would mingle in the crowd and disappear. Madanlal, the Punjabi refugee, was ready to act, in fact, ready to take revenge —an opportunity he had been longing for since he crossed the border as a vagrant without having anything other than the clothes he wore. Madanlal successfully primed and planted his gun cotton slab; in order to ensure that Karkare threw the hand grenades as soon as his ammunition exploded, Madanlal tried to bribe Chottu Ram, a driver staying in the Birla House servants' quarters, to allow them to approach the podium where the Mahatma was sitting, ostensibly to take photographs of the Mahatma. Chottu Ram became suspicious and wondered the need for photographing Bapu from the back especially when Madanlal was not carrying any camera. Madanlal walked off as if he was leaving the place, but instead went up to the wall behind the podium and ignited the fuse.

A loud explosion suddenly caused a pandemonium and the audience started running helter-skelter, but nothing followed thereafter. Karkare with his fingers wrapped tight around his hand grenade observed a stunned Badge was standing still! He had decided at the last minute not to act and advised Shankar to leave the place. Badge and Shankar merged with the crowd and made their way to the Hindu Mahasabha Bhawan where Badge had a showdown with Nathuram and Narayan later in the evening. Karkare also made a good escape.

Without any gun shot or grenade explosion being heard, bewildered Madanlal paused for few seconds and then realised that the plan was foiled. Now, the only option left was to run away. Sulochana Devi, a nearby neighbour who came looking for her three-year-old son Mahendra playing with other children in the servants' quarters saw Madanlal talking to Chottu Ram, placing the bomb on the wall, lighting the fuse and the bomb exploding. She identified Madanlal as the bomb to Ful Singh, the watchman at the Birla House, an armed policeman and a soldier, who first grabbed the fleeing Madanlal. On frisking Madanlal, another hand grenade was also found on his person. Utterly disappointed, Nathuram and Narayan, abandoning their accomplices rushed towards the waiting taxi while Gopal joined them—the assassination plot thus ended in a fiasco.

On interrogation, Madanlal confessed of being a part of the seven-member gang who on 20 January 1948 walked in the Birla House to kill the Mahatma, responsible for the miserable plight of the refugees, at his prayer meeting. In the late evening, Madanlal also led the police contingent to the Marina Hotel where Nathuram Godse and Narayan Apte had been staying under assumed names and also to Sharif Hotel and Hindu Mahasabha Bhawan where all other members of the squad were camping. Everyone left by that time and the police team was only able to recover some letters and a pile of laundry clothes which had the initials 'NVG' on it from the Room no 40, Marina Hotel.

With further revelations from Madanlal, the intelligence agencies came to know that the members of the team were from Maharashtra, and Madanlal himself boarded the train from Bombay. Among the gang members, he deliberately misspelt the name of his 'seth' as 'Kirkree'. Another lead the investigating agency got was Madanlal's boastful admission that being a refugee from West Punjab, he had the privilege of obtaining the blessings of none else other than Veer Savarkar, the great Hindu political leader.

Immediately after the primary interrogation of Madanlal, D J Sanjevi, the then head of police administration at Delhi sent an officer of the Delhi police to brief the CID in Bombay to unveil the conspiracy. Unfortunately, the secret plan was never unearthed, and the country became merely a dumb witness to the great tragedy of the century—Mahatma Gandhi was assassinated within the next ten days.

As for the Poona Brahmins duo, the 'Great killing' attempt suffered a major setback with Madanlal in custody. Besides being distressed by the failure, there was growing apprehension that Madanlal would open his mouth and reveal the rest of the details of the conspiracy.

Although the plotters left the city and were at large, the police could fruitfully decipher vital clues to trace them all while investigating the case. At Bombay, a CID source revealed that Madanlal's associate was a person named Karkare in Ahmednagar. Within the next few hours, Jamshed (Jimmy) Nagarwala, the then Deputy Commissioner, Special Branch, CID, Bombay, extracted the information of Vishnu Ramkrishna Karkare in detail, and also came to know about Digambar Ramchandra Badge, an arms dealer in Poona, his accomplice in the conspiracy.

A Delhi police officer left for Bombay without, however, waiting any longer for Madanlal's preliminary confession report to be typed and verified. He carried with himself all the previously accumulated information in the form of a mere mass of scribbles (a common practice in investigation), and unfortunately, he slipped by missing the *most* significant piece of information—the details of Godse that Madanlal had given out while making his confession.

On 24 January 1948, at about 9.30 pm, Madanlal, being unable to bear the custodial torture any longer, finally broke down and agreed to offer a full account of the conspiracy. It was a statement of 54 pages containing the detailed information about Karkare with correct spelling and particulars of his political antecedents, the location of Shastra Bhandar in Poona wherefrom the arms and ammunition were procured. Madanlal's account now bore more vivid descriptions of Godse and Apte, along with the location of *Hindu Rastriya*. Madanlal, however, got the spelling wrong, albeit inadvertently.

༺ৡৡ

Chitpawan Brahmins from Poona finally strike

With Madanlal making confessional statements, Godse and Apte, the would-be subjects of the most intensive manhunt in India's contemporary history, realised that time was closing on them. Haunted by the spectre of getting arrested, along with the irreparable sense of failure in accomplishing the *great job* for which they had so proudly vowed and collected donations, put the Chitpawan Brahmins into a situation from which escape became almost impossible.

A visibly upset Nathuram summoned his brother, Gopal, and on 26 January 1948 they met at the Thana station, near Bombay, where Karkare also joined the fragmented faction. Soon the group proceeded to meet Dada Maharaj, and also his brother Dixit Maharaj who were supposed to have provided them with one revolver, but their failure at the Birla House possibly prevented them from giving any.

'Police is after us,' whispered Nathuram in his strained voice. 'We failed because so many persons were involved,' he continued, 'this time, I will do it myself, Apte will be with me.' A dependable revolver was all that was required for the *great job* and the Brahmins duo frantically searched for a suitable one from one corner to another in the city of Bombay, but in vain. As time was closing on them, Nathuram decided to immediately leave Bombay for Delhi. Apte endorsed the idea with a hope of obtaining a revolver in one of the camps of the disgruntled refugees in the capital.

It was on 27 January 1948, Godse and Apte again boarded the Air India aircraft heading for Delhi in the morning. None of the make-shift camps in Delhi where the duo had rushed from the airport itself could oblige the conspirators. Fatigued by the day's ordeal, both the chief conspirators from Poona ultimately reached their temporary destination, Old Delhi Railway Retiring Room no 6 where Gopal and Karkare, already camping in Delhi, called on them.

Nathuram, Apte's last minute groundwork

'Only Doctor Saab can bail us out,' Apte sounded confident.

'You are right; let's not waste time. We will take the

earliest available train for Gwalior,' nodded Nathuram.

An old vanguard of the RSS, Dattatraya Parchure, the homeopath doctor at Gwalior, boastfully maintained a private army of more than 1,000 Hindu troopers which gained notoriety for slaughtering a compartment-full of Muslims fleeing from Bhopal to Delhi just after the Partition. A true zealot of Hindutva, Parchure whose passion was to rout the Muslims from the free India was more than happy to receive his beloved comrades who unexpectedly rang his door bell past midnight. The next 24 hours were a trying time for the duo who had been frantically looking for a revolver in Poona, Bombay, Delhi and ultimately in Gwalior. In the evening on the following day, their saga came to an end when Dr Parchure handed over a properly wrapped packet containing a black Beretta M1934 semi-automatic pistol in .380 ACP caliber, serial number 606824 and twenty rounds of ammunition. The Beretta, the killer firearm, was immediately hidden in Nathuram's bedroll and the Hindu protagonists took the last train leaving Gwalior for Delhi.

Nathuram was all set to strike again, finally, to take the life of Gandhiji, the ardent preacher of non-violence, and was checking at the last minute details with his repository assembled at the retiring Room no 6 at the Delhi railway station to make his *great mission* a success. It was a relaxed day for all of them. It appeared to them that they were getting very close to the finishing line.

'We can't afford to miss the opportunity; this may be the last one, who knows?' said Godse almost resigned to fate. 'We must have a full-proof arrangement,' he commanded confirming that the *great mission* would be executed on the following day, Friday, 30 January 1948.

A bomb explosion had taken place barely a few days back at the prayer meeting on 20 January 1948; the plotters would, therefore, be expected to have to negotiate intense police security. Since so many burqa clad women visited Gandhiji, a best way was to send Nathuram under the cover of a burqa since women were allowed closest to the leader. A burqa was bought from the nearby market; Nathuram tried it on but he was so uncomfortable that the plan was dumped. Another bright idea surfaced: Nathuram could disguise as a photographer. An old type camera would be required having a tripod with a black hood under which the photographer would operate, and the camera base would offer enough room to accommodate a pistol. Instantly, discarding the 'bright idea', Nathuram looked for other alternatives since no professional photographer would come with an age old camera for news coverage.

Friday, 30 January 1948 was, however, another busy day for Mahatma when, besides meeting the stream of visitors and media representatives, he had also finalised his last will and testament by which he recommended that the Congress Party should be dissolved and converted into a social organisation named the Lok Sevak Sangh. Another important task the undisputed leader had accomplished was to convince the Sardar Patel (he had decided to step down from the ministry) to forge a tie with Nehru, his main adversary, and remain in the cabinet to serve the nation. 'India would need both Nehru and Sardar,' confirmed Bapu to Sardar. Vallabhbhai had also vouched for his deep faith in Bapu and left the Birla House since it was time for Gandhiji to address the prayer meeting at 5.00 pm.

At the retiring room, the inevitable moment was slowly approaching at its own pace and the assassins were also getting ready for their final hunt. The reckless and ineluctable instrument of Savarkar's political animosity was ready with the arsenal; more sadistic and atrocious than cruelty itself. Nathuram was confident that even with a pistol having seven rounds of cartridges placed on his hip, he would, defying the security, manage to sneak inside the lawn of the Birla House. Apte and Karkare would mingle with the crowd in such a way that in case anyone tried to interfere when Godse would aim at his prey, the 'duo' would take proper care. Nathuram reminded his accomplices yet again the chalked out sequence of events while they were proceeding to their destination in a *tonga*.

It was already ten minutes past 5 o'clock when Gandhiji was slowly emerging at the lawn for the prayer meeting, leaning his two arms, as usual, leisurely on the shoulders of his two long time aides, Manu and Abha. A soft murmur went through the impatient gathering: 'Bapu, Bapu'.

'Namaste Gandhiji, you are late today' Bapuji's last greetings came from his assassin, Nathuram. 'Yes, I am . . .' before the champion of non-violence could utter his last words, all three shots from Nathuram's Baretta perforated the chest of the old fragile figure. Bapu's life did prove itself to be too fragile to sustain three shots fired at point black range. The bare residue was just an old, emaciated human form in loin-cloth still wriggling on the lap of arid dust that he walked upon a few seconds ago. Mahatma Gandhi had met with the end of his life on the prayer-ground; a clear demonstration of how grotesque humanity can sometimes be. Nathuram did not fail this time. An era came to an end.

Nathuram Godse's eyes must have shone with a strangely incomprehensible exultation. After firing the shots, he raised his hand with the gun and called for the police. He was apprehended. But even if the gory sight might have eventually filled Nathuram with incurable remorse, we do not know how Savarkar felt for the rest of his life.

In fact, Savarkar was one of the key persons the police had been looking for in connection with the explosion that took place earlier on 20 January 1948.

✍

The ultimate happens

It was a relaxed Friday evening, 30 January 1948, at around 6.00 pm, I was returning home from a friend's place. Surprisingly, the roads were nearly empty bearing a deserted look all around. Groups of people every-where, in small clusters, with anxious faces were talking in whispers. Many shops were hurriedly pulling down the shutters for a mysterious alarm. Streetlights did not glow. I was amazed. I came to know from a little girl that, 'Gandhiji is dead'. Instantly, I lost the presence of mind.

'Is it true?' I asked the grocer next to my house. 'Yes, Sir, Gandhiji has been shot dead. We have heard over the radio.'

Over the air came the grief-stricken voice of Panditji. '...the light has gone out of our lives and there is darkness everywhere. I do not know what to tell you and how to say it. Our beloved leader Bapu as we called him, the Father of the Nation, is no more.'

I could hardly think further. My heart was effortlessly crushed under an avalanche of feelings, myriad in colours and form. A mountain of grief heavily weighed on my head. Sorrow, disappointment and vexation swayed me at every turn. Maybe the associates of Madanlal had done the ultimate mischief. Had the conspiracy succeeded? But I had informed the Bombay Government well in advance. Such a big government, such an edifice of police force, such a mighty army; yet Mahatmaji had been shot dead!

In India's political history, the most fateful day soon turned out to be the blackest day. Bombay, the vibrant city, came to a complete halt with an aching sense of irreparable disaster. Soon the city took a deserted look of a 'bandh' (general strike). Every man, every woman, even the child was oppressed with grief. Did I say 'every'? No, here and there in the city itself, as it later became known, sweets were being distributed to celebrate the event!

∽

Ministers' threat

Next morning, the 31 January 1948, even on a 'bandh' day, I was determined to call on both B G Kher and Morarji Desai in the hope that they could, perhaps, tell me how it all had happened. B G Kher was leaving for Delhi to attend the funeral ceremony of Bapu, and he advised me to see Desai.

I again offered my services to Desai. 'It seems the conspirators are yet to be rounded up. They might even create further mischief,' I told the minister under a state of shock. 'If you think that my going to Delhi would be of any use to unearth the plot, I am ready to leave now.' I assured Desai yet again. 'You are right,' came the prompt reply. 'I shall write to Shankar, Secretary to Sardar Patel, and some police officer might be sent along with you.'

At night, I received a call from Morarji Desai. When I saw him the next morning, Desai gave me a little note and advised me to meet Nagarwala of the Special Branch, CID, Bombay.

Almost simultaneously, Nagarwala emerged in Desai's bungalow. 'We have not been able to prevent the heinous crime. It's a shame, but we would go through with post-mortem examination.' Nagarwala spoke in low voice. 'From Poona, I have gathered that you knew quite a lot regarding the crime.' Nagarwala told me in a stern cold voice. 'I promise to help you in all possible ways. On 21 January, I had already informed the Hon'ble Ministers everything I knew.' I assured the senior police officer once again.

'Well, what do you say about our putting you under arrest?' Nagarwala questioned.

'Why do you want to arrest me? I don't quite understand. Is it in connection with any crime or you want my assistance in the investigation?' I asked him with all humility.

Without replying Nagarwala said, 'We are afraid, if we do that, people might attack your house and rob you.' Looking straight at his eyes, I asserted, 'Be careful, Mr Nagarwala. You must think before you act.'

Nagarwala gazed at me attentively, perhaps to read my thoughts and after few seconds, noted down all my contact details in his personal diary, and then stood up to give me a parting military salute.

My interaction with Nagarwala made me both baffled and humiliated. Instead of taking my assistance in tracking the national enemies, why was he behaving so strangely?

After a couple of days, on 4 February 1948, I rang up the Premier, B G Kher and sought for an appointment. 'What can be done now? We were not present at Delhi but we had conveyed your message to the authorities in Delhi. What else . . . if you wish to talk, you can come and see me,' came the cold reply from the Premier.

A full-length portrait of Gandhiji caught my eye the moment I stepped into the visitors' room at the Premier's Bungalow. I saw B G Kher slowly approaching while chanting slokas from *Gita*. 'It was the will of God . . . somebody might come and kill me as well.' The Premier was in a mood to preach the teachings of *Gita*. 'You are a professor. If you can prepare a batch of twenty students who are ready to follow the principles of Mahatmaji and propagate his ideas, it will be a matter of great satisfaction.'

I did not wish to prolong the discussion and changing the topic I said, 'Your Deputy Commissioner was saying something about arresting me.'

'What can we do in this matter? He will do whatever he thinks proper' he cajoled me.

'But what would you say about the information I had given you beforehand?' I asked.

'Look, Professor. We don't know much about you. You might have been connected to the conspirators, and when you realised that you could not hold the secret any longer, perhaps you came and informed us.'

I felt indignant, but keeping my temper under control, I asked, 'Then did I trust you in vain?'

'No, we will see that you are not unnecessarily harassed. But you see, police will do whatever is necessary. We don't interfere with their job.' Kher emphasised.

'But, Sir, didn't I take risks and didn't I tell you that I was ready to go to Delhi. If only you had put me in contact with Madanlal, maybe, the whole conspiracy would have been revealed. We could have averted this calamity'. I submitted before the Premier.

When I was about to leave the Premier's bungalow, Morarji Desai walked in. Kher saw him, looked at me and said, 'If you have any question, you can ask him,' and in the same breath, he told Desai, 'Look, this gentleman is charging us of negligence.'

Morarji immediately lost his temper and shouted at me, 'You are one of the conspirators. You have been helping Madanlal. I will have you locked up.' B G Kher, who was once preaching the philosophy of Gita, said, 'Now see. You shouldn't have said all this to me.'

Did I really deserve such vile words just because I had tried to save the life of the Father of the Nation? I had approached the ministers for all that I came to know about the conspiracy and such was the result! I veered my mind and thought retrospectively for a moment. When I was a student, I used to study the writings of Mahatmaji with great devotion. For wearing a Gandhi cap, a symbolic allegiance to the Indian freedom movement, I had to resign as a teacher from a high school in Ajmer, a city in the erstwhile Rajputana, now in

Rajasthan. I had given up my college studies for my participation in the National Movement in 1930, and again I had undergone the sufferings of jail life in the 'Quit India Movement' of 1942. In response to the appeal issued by Maulana Abul Kalam Azad in 1947, I had sent in my name to Prof Humayun Kabir, his secretary, to work as a volunteer to propagate Gandhian teachings to bring peace in Western UP which was being ravaged with communal riots. Did I not try to exterminate all feelings of communalism whenever I had heard refugees abusing Gandhiji. Yet, the ministers were trying to implicate me in the Bapu murder conspiracy!

I did not know from where I had gained the inner-strength to counteract the erring minister. Perhaps, the philosophy of Gandhiji's *Satyagraha* stood me in a firm stead. As soon as Morarji Desai stopped, I replied, 'Do you try to frighten me with your threats? Even if you put me behind the bars, I will make it known to everybody that I had given you the information well in advance, and that you have failed yourself to save Bapu. Having confidence in you, I had given you all the vital information, and you are now saying that I am a party to this conspiracy? It is not at all expected from responsible people like you, Sir.'

Morarji Desai came back to sense. 'If I had considered you as a conspirator, I would have got you arrested long back. But this is not the case. In fact, when the Delhi Police tried to blame my police, we told them that whatever information we got from you, we had conveyed the same to the authorities in Delhi. So, it was not our fault.'

I could understand that now the search was on to find a scapegoat, and I would not be surprised if it should be myself. I had no strength to come back. My heart had become heavy and I could not think further. I did not remember how I dragged myself out of the Premier's bungalow.

'You are one of the conspirators. You have been helping Madanlal. I will have you locked up.' These words kept ringing in my ears. Being engrossed in these thoughts, I took a bus without knowing which direction it was heading for. Almost mechanically, I reached Ruia College where a large crowd of students had assembled for a condolence meeting for Mahatmaji. I did not know how I could address my own students. If Gandhiji were invisibly present, he would have wept at the behaviour of his ardent followers.

On 17 February 1948, in the morning while I was taking a bath, my wife told me that a CID officer had come to see me. I was certain that the officer had arrived with a warrant of arrest, and I should prepare myself to spend my days in confinement. I had offered my Pujas (a form of Hindu worship), albeit in a hurry and bidding goodbye to my wife, I greeted the officer.

'Well, let's go!'

'No, Professor, we are here to record your statement.'

'But, I have already given my statement to both the Premier and Morarji Desai.' I assured the young officer.

'Sir, a case for the murder of Gandhiji would be put in the court soon and you will have to be there to give your evidence. But before that we will record your statement.'

In my statement, the junior officer refused to record the names of either B G Kher or Morarji Desai. I did vehemently object to this, and ultimately, 'high-authorities' was included in place of 'the ministers of

Bombay'. After a few days, I was produced before the Chief Presidency Magistrate, Bombay and my brief statement was documented. I was also asked to identify the culprits. All the others who were present there included taxi drivers, hotel managers and attendants, religious heads and factory owners. Some of them had helped the culprits with money, some with arms and ammunition and some had given them shelter. It was a massive conspiracy that slowly unfolded at the trial.

ल॰)

Sardar Patel in dock

After the great tragedy of 30 January 1948, a nationwide fury followed with Sardar Vallabhbhai Patel, the then Home Minister, in the firing line for not being able to save the life of the Mahatma. In a meeting convened by the Congress Party to mark the sense of horror and sorrow at Gandhiji's death, Jayaprakash Narayan, the socialist exponent in the Congress party, stressed that Patel could not escape the responsibility for the assassination, and demanded an explanation for not taking any special measures especially when there was open propaganda inciting people to murder Gandhiji and a bomb had actually been hurled at him 10 days prior to the fateful day.

As reflected by Pyarelal, the secretary of Mahatma Gandhi, it was true that Gandhiji had summarily rejected a proposal to scan every person coming to his prayer meeting.[13] Acting on the information received from Bombay, Patel, in fact had ordered tightening of security measures. Gandhiji rejected this since his faith did not allow him to accept any kind of human protection at the prayer time when he put himself under the sole protection of God.

What was baffling, however, was that in spite of having definite and concrete information about the conspiracy, the authorities failed to trace and arrest the conspirators and frustrate their plan when all the members of the squad had entered the scene from the same front entrance. In fact, the failure showed the extent of the rot that had penetrated many branches of the security services, not excluding the police. Later it was brought to light that the RSS had entry even to government departments, and many police officials, not to mention the rank and file, had sympathies and also actively helped those engaged in RSS activities. Nehru took the brunt of the situation and he cautioned the then Home Minister, Vallabhbhai Patel, on 26 February 1948 that, 'The RSS has infiltrated our offices and the police force and therefore official secrecy cannot be maintained.'[14]

At the time of Partition, the RSS, an archrival of the Congress, was directly attributing the division of India to Gandhiji's *Muslim appeasement policy* where the country witnessed a huge influx of Hindu and Sikh refugees cursing the Congress and Gandhiji, in particular, for their frightful plight. Even before the bomb explosion on 20 January 1948, some of the refugee camps in Delhi were known to be buzzing with the talk of assassination of Gandhiji and other Congress leaders who enjoyed the reputation of being opposed to communalistic ideologies. Mahatma's tragic end in the hands of an extremist Hindu group further aggravated the already charged atmosphere resulting in a ban imposed on the RSS and the prominent RSS functionaries including Madhav Sadashivrao Golwalkar, then *Sanghachalak*, the chief of the organisation, were detained.

In the wake of Gandhiji's assassination, on 1 February 1948, Sardar Patel had, however, appealed to the people not to succumb to unworthy reactions. The *Indian Express* carried the appeal on the following day, 'Sardar Patel, the Deputy Prime Minister, tonight appealed to all sections of people to keep calm. He said that he was distressed to learn that in some places in Bombay and Madras misguided members of the public had indulged in acts of violence against members of Hindu Mahasabha and RSS. 'We shall prove ourselves unworthy of Mahatma Gandhi's teachings and his trust in us if we yield to feelings of revenge,' he said. – API.

In his broadcast to the nation after the assassination on 30 January 1948, Nehru said: 'A mad man has put an end to his life, for I can only call him mad who did it, and yet there has been enough poison spread in this country during the past years and months, and this poison has had an effect on people's minds. We must face this poison, and we must face all the perils that encompass us, and face them not madly or badly but rather in the way that our beloved teacher taught us to face them.'[15] Later in a meeting in Ramlila Grounds, Delhi, he again emphasised: 'What we have to see is how and why even one man among 400 millions could cause this terrible wound on our country. How an atmosphere was created in which people like him could act in that manner and yet dare to call themselves Indians.'[16] Nehru was, however, all along sceptical about the RSS and even couple of days prior to the great tragedy, speaking at a public rally at Amritsar in Punjab, the Prime Minister had warned, 'The RSS had done immense harm to the country; it would be stamped out.'[17]

Pandit Nehru identified the 'poison' rooted in the RSS when 26 February 1948 in a letter to Sardar Patel he asserted, 'More and more I have come to the conclusion that Bapu's murder was not an isolated business but part of a much wider campaign organised chiefly by the RSS.'[18] In a prompt reply which reached Nehruji on the very next day, 27 February 1948, Patel made a categorical statement saying, 'I have kept myself almost in daily touch with the progress of the investigations regarding Bapu's assassination case . . . All the main accused have given long and detailed statements of their activities. It also clearly emerges from the statements that the RSS was not involved in it at all.' Contrary to his other colleagues in the party, all through Patel who was accredited as the 'Iron man of India', held a different view of the RSS. Only a few days before the gruesome murder when the RSS ferocity was sweeping the country, at a public meeting in Lucknow on 6 January 1948, Patel declared,

'In the Congress those who are in power feel that by virtue of their authority they will be able to crush the RSS. You cannot crush an organisation by using the *danda*. The *danda* is meant for thieves and dacoits. After all the RSS men are not thieves and dacoits. They are patriots who love their country.'

It was a privilege for me to have access to certain secret intelligence documents which strongly suggest that even if the RSS was not implicated directly by Sardar Vallabhbhai Patel, the then Home Minister, Madhav Sadashiv Golwalkar, the then RSS *Sanghachalak*, was not entirely averse to such a happening. On 6 December, 1947, Golwalkar convened a meeting of RSS workers in the town of Govardhan, not far from Delhi. The police report on this meeting says it discussed how to 'assassinate the leading persons of the Congress in order to terrorise the public and to get a hold over them.'

Two days later, Golwalkar addressed a crowd of several thousand volunteers at the Rohtak Road Refugee Camp in Delhi. The police reporter in attendance wrote that the RSS leader said that 'the Sangh will not rest until it had finished Pakistan. If anyone stood in our way we will have to finish them too, whether it was Nehru Government or any other Government . . .' Referring to Muslims, he said that no power on earth could keep them in Hindustan. They will have to quit this country . . .' If they were made to stay here the responsibility would be the Government's and the Hindu community would not be responsible. Mahatma Gandhi could not mislead them any longer. We have the means whereby [our] opponents could be immediately silenced.'

Contrary to Gandhiji's characterising the RSS as a 'communal body with a totalitarian outlook' and compared their 'discipline, courage and capacity for hard work' with those of Hitler's Nazis and the Fascists under Mussolini, Patel viewed that the members of the RSS as 'patriots, though misguided,' and in a letter to Golwalkar, Patel's blanket offer for the RSS members to join Congress was significant. Sardar Patel was, perhaps, the lone Congressman whose sympathy to RSS was known as a common secret, after whose death Hindu Mahasabha unanimously and solemnly passed a resolution expressing profound sorrow on the sad demise of the staunch, Hindu-minded Bismark of Bharat—Sardar Vallabhbhai Patel. The resolution was placed before the Assembly, and moved by the Hindu Rashtrapati, Dr Khare himself, who said, 'We are not so narrow-minded as the Congressmen who did not utter even a word of sympathy, and sorrow on the passing away of Dharmaveer Dr Moonjee and Shri N C Kelkar, the Hindu Mahasabha leaders who, one time, were the loyal lieutenants of the Congress itself. On the other hand, we Mahasabhaites cancelled the presidential procession to express our respect and reverence towards the Sardar.'

꧁꧂

Post Murder legal process begins

Immediately after the sad demise of the 'Father of the Nation', based on the statement of Shri Nand Lal Mehta, an FIR was lodged with the Tughlak Road Police Station, Delhi and the English translation of the original FIR of Mahatma Gandhi Assassination case—1948 appears on p.72.

Statement of Shri Nand Lal Mehta:

> Today I was present at Birla House. Around ten minutes past five in the evening, Mahatma Gandhi left his room in Birla House for the Prayer Ground. Sister Abha Gandhi and sister Sanno Gandhi were accompanying him. Mahatma was walking with his hands on the shoulders of the two sisters. Two

more girls were there in the group. I along with Lala
Brij Kishan, a silver merchant, resident of No. 1,
Narendra Place, Parliament Street and Sardar
Gurbachan Singh, resident of Timar Pur, Delhi were
also there. Apart from us, women from the Birla
household and two or three members of the staff
were also present. Having crossed the garden,
Mahatma climbed the concrete steps towards the
prayer place. People were standing on both sides
and approximately three feet of vacant space was
left for the Mahatma to pass through. As per
custom, the Mahatma greeted the people with
folded hands. He had barely covered six or seven
steps when a person whose name I learnt later as
Narayan Vinayak Godse, resident of Poona,
stepped closer and fired three shots from a pistol
at the Mahatma from barely 2 to 3 feet distance
which hit the Mahatma in his stomach and chest and
blood started flowing. Mahatmaji fell backwards,
uttering 'Raam–Raam'. The assailant was apprehended on the spot with the weapon. The Mahatma
was carried away in an unconscious state towards
the residential unit of the Birla House where he
passed away instantly and the police took away the
assailant.

Sd/-
N L Mehta/30.1.1948

Having received the information I rushed to the Birla
House to find the dead body of the Mahatma at room
No. 3. Met Shri Nand Lal Mehta, his statement recorded
and got confirmed after reading it out to him. Copy of

the statement handed over to him. Came to know that the assailant was whisked away by the Assistant Sub-Inspector. It was a case of Section 302 Indian Penal Code. All the case papers were sent to the Police Station Tughlak Road and I got engaged in conducting investigations. A special report may be forwarded through the police station.

Sd. in English/30 January 1948

First Information of a Cognizable Crime
Reported under Section 154 Criminal Procedure Code

Police Station: Tughlak Road No. : 68	District: Central
1 Date and hour when reported	Date and hour of occurence: 30.1.1948/5:45 P.M.
2 Name and residence of informant/ complainant	Shri Nand Lal Mehta, son of Shri Natha Lal Mehta, Indian, Building Lala Suraj Prasad M Block, ConnaughtCircus
3 Brief description of offence (with section) and of property carried off, if any	302 I.P.C.
4 Place of occurrence and distance/direction from Police Station	Birla House, distance 2 furlongs
5 Name and address of the criminal	
6 Steps taken regarding investigation/explanation of delay in recording information	

Prosecution process starts

A Special Court was constituted under notification no 54/1/48-Political, Government of India, Ministry of Home Affairs, dated 4 May 1948, u/s 10 and 11 of the Bombay Public Security Measures Act, 1947, as extended to the Province of Delhi, and the Gandhi Murder Case was made over to the Court for trial, under notification no 54/1/48-Political, Government of India, Ministry of Home Affairs, dated 13 May 1948.

Atma Charan Agrawal, ICS was appointed as the Judge. All the accused persons were brought to Delhi before the commencement of the trial, and were lodged in the Red Fort in a specially selected area, which was declared to be a 'prison' under notification no 54/6/48-Political, Government of India, Ministry of Home Affairs, dated 15 May 1948.

It was 27 May 1948 on which Mahatma Gandhi Murder Trial was commenced at the Red Fort, Delhi. In Delhi, the Red Fort happened to be a citadel which had witnessed historical trials in colonised India. Bahadur Shah Jafar, the last Mughal and others accused of waging the War of Independence against the British in 1857 were the first to be tried in the fort. Netaji Subhas Chandra Bose, the commander of the Indian National Army, was next to be brought to trial to deal with the charge of sedition and revolt against the Second World War. The third was to be for the assassination of Mahatma Gandhi, the Father of the Nation.

A row of cells in one of the walls of the fort was turned into a jail for the accused. Twelve persons were accused on different charges, and three of them were absconding. The nine produced before Atma Charan on

27 May 1948 and onward were (1) Nathuram Vinayak Godse, (aged 37), Poona, (2) Narayan Dattatreya Apte, (34), Poona, (3) Vishnu Ramkrishna Karkare, (37), Ahmednagar, (4) Madanlal Kishanlal Pahwa, (20), Bombay (originally from District Montgomery, Pakistan) (5) Shankar Kistaiya, (20), Solapur, (6) Gopal Vinayak Godse, (27), Poona, (7) Digambar Ramchandra Badge, (40), Poona, (8) Vinayak Damodar Savarkar, (66), Bombay, and (9) Dattatraya Sadashiv Parchure, (47) Gwalior.

The three absconding persons were (1) Gangadhar Dandavate, (2) Gangadhar Jadhao, and (3) Suryadeo Sharma, all from Gwalior.

Digambar Badge was an accused, but later turned approver. Thus Savarkar was subsequently made accused no 7 in the serial.

All the accused were charged with criminal conspiracy, (120B), murder (302) and various other sections under the Indian Penal Code, Indian Arms Act, Explosive Substances Act. Atma Charan, the Special Judge, read out, explained and the charge sheets were handed over to the accused present who themselves pleaded 'not guilty' and expressed their desire to be tried.

Nathuram Godse, the main accused, and Vinayak Damodar Savarkar, accused of being one of the chief conspirators, made detailed statements.

Narayan Apte, accused no 2, had B Sc and B T degrees and was a popular teacher hailing from Ahmednagar, a District place, 70 miles off Poona, where Karkare, accused no 3, was residing. Both Apte and Karkare came in touch with each other in their activities of common interest—organising the Hindus. Apte had also started a rifle club to train the youth in the use of fire arms.

It was 28 March 1944 on which date Apte and Nathuram had jointly launched the 'Agrani', a Marathi daily from Poona for propagating the cause of Hindu Sanghatan (organisation). Subsequently, following a ban, 'Agrani' was rechristened to the 'Hindu Rashtra' in 1946. The last issue of the daily on 31 January 1948 carried the news of Gandhi's assassination and mentioned the name of the assassin, Nathuram V Godse, who was the editor of *Hindu Rashtra*. Apte and Nathuram Godse worked together for 5 to 6 years under the banner of the Hindu Mahasabha.

Apte, a close confidant of Nathuram, was present both on 20 and 30 January 1948 on the spot at Delhi along with Nathuram, and the prosecution described him as the main brain behind the conspiracy.

Vishnu Karkare, an active political worker of the RSS, was the owner of Deccan Guest House at Ahmednagar. When burning Noakhali in East Bengal had become the slaughter house of the Hindus residing there, Karkare, with a batch of ten, had gone there to mobilise the Hindus and adopt a militant posture in their defence under the Hindu Mahasabha banner. Karkare was also present on the spot on both 20 and 30 January 1948 at Delhi.

Madanlal, who had exploded the gun-cotton slab at the Birla House on 20 January 1948, was a refugee. A witness to the horrified events of massacre, loot and arson, Madanlal, with a view to justifying his deeds, had narrated his miserable plights in his statement before the Court.

Shankar Kistaiya, accused no 5 was the servant of Digambar Badge, the approver. Shankar was in Delhi on the spot on 20 January 1948.

Gopal Godse, accused no 6, was a brother of Nathuram V Godse. Gopal, an employee in the Ordnance Department, had gone overseas during the Second World War and on return he was posted in Khadaki Military Store Depot near Poona. Gopal was charged with conspiracy as he was present at the Birla House on 20 January 1948.

Digambar Badge a Hindu *Sanghatanist* (organiser), who had eventually turned into an approver, was an arms dealer and he had achieved his notoriety for marketing bullet-proof vests. Badge held the view that Hindus should be armed in the pockets in which they were in minority and be able to retaliate in case of any attack from the Muslims. It was claimed that Badge had supplied the gun-cotton slab ignited by Madanlal, and other ammunition. He was present on the spot on 20 January 1948 at Delhi.

Accused no 8, Dr D S Parchure, was a homoeopath doctor practising at Gwalior. An able Hindu organiser, Parchure had met attacks by the Muslims with counter-attacks. He was involved in the Gandhi Murder Case on the charge that Nathuram had obtained the revolver from him.

Murder trial begins

C K Daphtary, Advocate General of Bombay, appeared as Chief Public Prosecutor, and was assisted by N K Petigara, M G Vyavaharkar, J C Shah and Jwala Prasad.

Savarkar was represented by L B Bhopatkar, Jumnadas Mehta, Ganpat Rai, K L Bhopatkar, B Banerji, J P Mitter and N P Aiyer.

On 24 June 1948, the trial court started recording the prosecution evidence which continued until 6 November 1948. In all, 149 witnesses came to court, and their evidence consisted of 720 pages having 404 documentary exhibits and 80 material exhibits.

On 8 November 1948, the recording of the statements of the accused began and continued till 22 November 1948, and their statements consisted of 106 pages. All the accused except Shankar Kistaiya filed written statements consisting of 297 pages.

On 1 December 1948, the hearing of the arguments started which continued till 30 December 1948.

Charges framed

On hearing both the prosecution and the defence counsels, Atma Charan framed the charges reading as under:

FIRSTLY
NATHURAM V GODSE, NARAYAN D APTE, VISHNU R KARKARE, MADANLAL K PAHWA, SHANKAR KISTAIYA, GOPAL V GODSE, VINAYAK D SAVARKAR AND DATTATRAYA S PARCHURE between 1 December 1947 and 30 January 1948, at Poona, Bombay, Delhi and other places agreed and conspired among and between yourselves and Digambar R Badge who has been tendered a pardon, Gangadhar S Dandavate, Gangadhar

Jadhav and Suryadeo Sharma, who along with others not known are absconding, to do or cause to be done an illegal act viz., to commit the murder of Mohandas Karamchand Gandhi, more popularly known as 'Mahatma Gandhi,' and the same act viz., the murder of 'Mahatma Gandhi' was done in pursuance of the said agreement and conspiracy at Delhi on 30 January 1948, and thereby committed an offence punishable under Section 120 B of the Indian Penal Code read with Section 302 of the Indian Penal Code and within the cognisance of the Court;

SECONDLY
That in pursuance of the said agreement and conspiracy between 10 and 20 January 1948 and you, NATHURAM V GODSE, NARAYAN D APTE, VISHNU R KARKARE, MADANLAL K PAHWA, SHANKAR KISTAIYA, GOPAL V GODSE along with Digambar R Badge,

A (1) transported without a licence to Delhi arms and ammunition viz., 2 revolvers with cartridges, in contravention of the provisions of Section 10 of the Indian Arms Act and thereby committed an offence punishable under Section 19(d) of the Indian Arms Act and within the cognisance of the Court;

(2) abetted each other in the commission of the above offence and thereby committed an offence punishable under Section 19(d) of the Indian Arms Act read with Sections 109 and 114 of the Indian Penal Code, and within the cognisance of the Court;

B (1) at Delhi, had without a licence in your possession and under your control arms and ammunition, viz., 2 revolvers with cartridges, in contravention of the provisions of Section 14 and 15 of the Indian Arms Act and thereby committed an offence punishable under Section 19(f) of the Indian Arms Act and within the cognisance of the Court;

(2) at Delhi, abetted each other in the commission of the above offence and thereby an offence punishable under Section 19(f) of the Indian Arms Act read with Sections 109 and 114 of the Indian Penal Code, and within the cognisance of the Court;

THIRDLY

That in pursuance of the said agreement and conspiracy between 10 and 20 January 1948 at Delhi you NATHURAM V GODSE, NARAYAN D APTE, VISHNU R KARKARE, MADANLAL K PAHWA, SHANKAR KISTAIYA, GOPAL V GODSE along with Digambar R Badge

A (1) had in your possession and under your control explosive substances, viz., 2 guncotton-slabs and 5 hand-grenades with detonators and wicks, with intent to endanger life by means thereof or to enable any other person to endanger life by means thereof and thereby committed an offence punishable under section 4(b) of the Explosive Substances Act and within the cognisance of the Court;

(2) abetted each other in the commission of the
     above offence and thereby committed an
     offence punishable under section 4(b) of the
     Explosive Substances Act read with Section
     6 of the Act and within the cognisance of the
     Court;

B (1) had in your possession and under your
       control explosive substances, viz., 2 gun-
       cotton-slabs and 5 hand-grenades with
       detonators and wicks, under such circum-
       stances as to give rise to a reasonable
       suspicion that you did not have them in your
       possession or under your control for a lawful
       object and thereby committed an offence
       punishable under section 5 of the Explosive
       Substances Act and within the cognisance of
       the Court;

(2) abetted each other in the commission of the
     above offence and thereby committed an
     offence punishable under section 5 of the
     Explosive Substances Act read with Section
     6 of the Act and within the cognisance of the
     Court;

FOURTHLY

That in pursuance of the said agreement and
conspiracy between 10 and 20 January 1948 at Delhi
you

A (1) MADAN LAL K PAHWA—Unlawfully and
       maliciously caused an explosive substance
       viz., a gun cotton-slab, to explode, which
       explosion was of a nature likely to endanger

life and to cause serious injury to property
and thereby committed an offence punishable under section 3 of the Explosive
Substances Act and within the cognisance of
the Court;

(2) NATHURAM V GODSE, NARAYAN D APTE,
     VISHNU R KARKARE, MADANLAL K
     PAHWA, SHANKAR KISTAIYA, GOPAL V
     GODSE—along with Digambar R Badge
     abetted Madanlal K Pahwa in the
     commission of the above offence and thereby
     committed an offence punishable under
     section 3 of the Explosive Substances Act
     read with Section 6 of the Act and within the
     cognisance of the Court;

FIFTHLY
That in pursuance of the said agreement and
conspiracy on 20 January 1948 at the Birla House,
Delhi, you NATHURAM V GODSE, NARAYAN D
APTE, VISHNU R KARKARE, MADANLAL K
PAHWA, SHANKAR KISTAIYA, GOPAL V GODSE,
VINAYAK D SAVARKAR—along with Digambar R
Badge abetted each other in the commission of an
offence viz., to commit the murder of 'Mahatma
Gandhi' which offence is punishable with death or
transportation for life and which offence was not
committed in consequence of the abetment and
thereby committed an offence punishable under
Section 115 of the Indian Penal Code read with
section 302 of the Indian Penal Code and within the
cognisance of the Court;

SIXTHLY

That in pursuance of the said agreement and conspiracy between 28 and 30 January 1948, you

A (1) NATHURAM V GODSE AND NARAYAN D APTE—brought without a licence from Gwalior to Delhi arms and ammunition, viz., Automatic Pistol No 606824 with cartridges, in contravention of Section 6 of the Indian Arms Act and thereby committed an offence punishable under Section 19(c) of the Indian Arms Act and within the cognisance of the Court;

(2) NATHURAM V GODSE, NARAYAN D APTE AND DATTATRAYA S PARCHURE—abetted each other in the commission of the above offence and thereby committed an offence punishable under Section 19(c) of the Indian Arms Act read with Section 114 of the Indian Penal Code and within the cognisance of the Court;

B (1) NATHURAM V GODSE—at Delhi, had in your possession and under your control arms and ammunition, viz., Automatic Pistol No 606824 with cartridges, in contravention of Sections 14 and 15 of the Indian Arms Act and thereby committed an offence punishable under Section 19(f) of the Indian Arms Act and within the cognisance of the Court;

(2) NARAYAN D APTE AND VISHNU R KARKARE at Delhi, abetted each other in the commission of the above offence and thereby committed an offence punishable under Section 19(f) of the Indian Arms Act read

with Section 114 of the Indian Penal Code and within the cognisance of the Court;

SEVENTHLY
That in pursuance of the said agreement and conspiracy on 30 January 1948 at the Birla House, Delhi you

A (1) NATHURAM V GODSE did commit murder by intentionally and knowingly causing the death of 'Mahatma Gandhi' and thereby committed an offence punishable under Section 302 of the Indian Penal Code and within the cognisance of the Court;

(2) NARAYAN D APTE AND VISHNU R KARKARE abetted Nathuram V Godse in the commission of the above offence, which offence was committed in your presence, and thereby committed an offence punishable under Section 302 of the Indian Penal Code read with Section 114 of the Indian Penal Code and within the cognisance of the Court;

(3) MADANLAL K PAHWA, SHANKAR KISTAIYA, GOPAL V GODSE, VINAYAK D SAVARKAR AND DATTATRAYA S PARCHURE —along with Digambar R Badge abetted Nathuram V Godse in the commission of the above offence, which offence was committed in your presence, and thereby committed an offence punishable under Section 302 of the Indian Penal Code read with Section 109 of the Indian Penal Code and within the cognisance of the Court.

The accused pleaded 'not guilty' and 'claimed to be tried'. Dattatraya S Parchure further pleaded that he was a subject of the Gwalior State and that, as such, he was not amenable to the jurisdiction of the Court.

∽

Godse's Trial

Atma Charan, the Special Judge, had taken his seat. An intense silence prevailed in the courtroom. The accused were seated in their respective seats in the dock. Counsels on either side were present. The reporters were ready holding their pens and notebooks.

It was 8 November 1948. The courtroom was packed to its capacity. People with special passes were the only ones who were allowed to enter. Now the defence of Nathuram Godse, the Accused no 1, was going to be heard.

The Judge started examination of the accused under Section 342 of the Criminal Procedure Code. He announced:

'Accused no 1, Nathuram Vinayak Godse, Hindu, age 37 years, Editor, Hindu Rashtra, Poona.'

Nathuram was up on his legs immediately after hearing 'accused no 1'.

'You have heard' the Judge continued, 'the entire evidence produced on behalf of the prosecution as against you. What have you got to say with regard to it?'

'I am to submit my written statement, Your Honour', Nathuram replied.

'Go ahead, read your statement' said the Judge. At this stage C K Daphtary, the Advocate General who was the Chief Prosecution Counsel stood up to object. He said, 'Your Honour, the accused may be allowed to depose only what is consistent with this case. Otherwise, he may not be allowed to read his statement.'

∽

Judge overruled the objection

Nathuram stood poised before the microphone to read out from his written statement. The silence that had so long been dominating in the courtroom was accentuated by the hollow echo of Godse's stentorian voice that soon reverberated around the hall.

Godse's final speech moved almost all those who were present in the hall, particularly the ladies who were shedding tears and wiping their eyes. Arguing his own case for the consecutive seven days, Nathuram Godse concluded his submissions with eulogies to the court that it was the only place left in India where bribery and favouritism did not exist. Godse pleaded to the judges that he had never put any appeal for himself nor would he ever ask for mercy because he had shown no mercy to the Great Man of India he had killed. The only favour he wanted was the permission to have a stroll sometimes during the day from his confined cell in the jail measuring about 8' X 10' which meant a slow death for him. He requested the court that either he should be executed immediately or permitted to leave his cell for a short time in the evening.

∽

Prosecution arguments against Nathuram and Apte

Pointing out the convincing evidence against Nathuram V Godse to the special judge Atma Charan, Daphtary said that not only Nathuram V Godse was guilty of the assassination of Mahatma Gandhi, he was also guilty of being an active accomplice to the party of conspirators who had plotted the assassination. Daphtary deduced from all sets of evidence that both the incidents of 20 January and 30 January 1948—the bomb explosion and the (subsequent) murder of Mahatma Gandhi respectively —were actually linked and the events were merely separate parts of the same transaction.

Nathuram V Godse's own statement, as Daphtary contended, betrayed the fact that he himself had under-taken the heinous and abhorrent task of taking the life of Mahatma Gandhi, and in justification of such an execrable act he said that in his opinion Gandhi was not doing the 'right' thing by being excessively supportive to the myriad interests of the minority community in the dominion of India.

Daphtary concluded staying that the murder being a political murder, and that no human being had the right to murder any one, Nathuram Godse was definitely culpable. He also submitted the corroborative statement that all deeds of Mahatma Gandhi had occurred well before 20 January 1948: his covenant of the payment of Rs 550 millions to Pakistan was made before 20 January 1948 implying that there could be no grave and sudden incitement which might have led Nathuram V Godse to commit the murder of Mahatma Gandhi. Daphtary also pointed out that Godse's statement attested to the fact that it was a pre-meditated murder, and that the delinquent committed the murder consciously and purposely.

As regards Narayan D Apte, a confederate in the conspiratorial league who had abetted Nathuram V Godse in the assassination, C K Daphtary said that Narayan Apte had formerly averred that they wanted to 'stage a demonstration' at the prayer-meeting on 20 January 1948, but regrettably enough the microphone was not working and thus making it impossible for them to 'stage' any such public meeting on that day. Besides, he had also affirmed that he had made certain arrangements with 'some' people with the design to bring refugee volunteers who, however, did not turn up. The entire design had gone awry, and, as Daphtary concluded, whether the situation, as Apte held it out to be, was jinxed or not, it lay with the accused himself to produce appropriate evidence to substantiate his plea.

Moreover, Daphtary maintained that Apte had also set out that he was in Bombay on 30 January 1948 and that he had actually telephoned to a particular person besides consulting Jamnadas Mehta. The Chief Prosecution Counsel opined that this information he affirmed only to 'be' a meet testament to his 'off-beat' role in the conspiracy. Daphtary said that if that were so, he could well be asked to give suitable and consequential evidence. Since lack of any such proof was definitely a case in point, the present situation could be described as an instance where a person could have been called to justify the point made but was not done. It was, therefore, evident that the court could very well draw an inference.

Despite the plea of alibi put forward by Apte, of which no such attempt had been made to prove the point, Daphtary submitted that the Prosecution had led evidence which showed that Apte was in Delhi both on 29 and 30 January 1948. It was also made clear by the Prosecution that since Narayan Apte had alleged that he was in Bombay on 30 and 31 January 1948, the burden of proving the plea did solely rest with the accused.

Next came the question of the two letters that were asseverated by Nathuram V Godse to have been sent by his own self along with his photo from Delhi on 30 January 1948 to Narayan Apte. In accordance with what he said, one of the two missives was sent to the Hindu Rashtra office and the other to his house. It was mentioned in his letter that he had sent the letter and the photo to others also. Godse had further alleged that the letter and the photo that were sent to others had been impounded by the police. Daphtary debunked this as spurious and desiccated and said that no one had been produced in the court either to bring forward the letter and the photo or to say that any one received a letter and a photo from Nathuram Godse and that it had been seized by the police. Adhering to such a view, he concluded that if Narayan Apte had any such letter from Nathuram Godse and if he had thought that such a letter was of some importance, there could have been no good reason why he should not have kept it to himself.

As regards Nathuram Godse's photograph, Daphtary said that in the cross-examination, the police photographer had stated that Godse's photo appeared to have been taken by a street photographer about two or three years ago although Nathuram Godse himself had declared that the photograph was taken sometime in

January 1948. Thus, if the police photographer's evidence was correct, the alleged series of events regarding the two letters and the photographs seemed to be just another deceitful scheme. Daphtary viewed that he would not admit that the post mark on the envelope was 30 January 1948. The letter, he added, was written by someone with the intention of creating a story which had been put forward.

Karkare's fate

Daphtary next dealt with the evidences against Vishnu R Karkare. Referring to a letter said to have been written by Karkare to Badge on 20 May 1947, he said that in that letter Karkare had asked Badge to send him some 'books', and in one section of his letter he bid Rs 150 for each 'book'. Daphtary here veered away from the concerned letter to what Digambar R Badge, the arms trafficker, had stated in his deposition. Daphtary pointed out that Vishnu Karkare wanted to buy hand-grenades from Badge, and thus by 'books' he had actually and most definitely meant it to be read as 'hand-grenades'. The 'book' and 'books' had been a common term between the confederates and meant to keep the identity of the real and more dangerous object veiled, undetected in case the letter fell into wrong hands. Daphtary also submitted that the letter corroborated what Badge had stated in his sworn evidence, on the point that Badge and Karkare were well acquainted with each other and, that the hand-writing expert had testified that letter was in the handwriting of Karkare himself.

❧

My evidence

C K Daphtary, the Chief Prosecution Counsel, initiated the proceedings saying that the fourth accused Madanlal had met Prof Jain at Bombay on or about 12 January 1948 and gave some inklings of the purpose of his going to Delhi. Prof Jain had never taken Madanlal seriously, and naturally, nobody would have. Prof Jain had, however, made a general effort to dissuade Madanlal, but in vain. It was declared that Prof Jain would be brought before the court for his deposition.

On 5 August 1948, I was produced in the Witness Box. 'I swear by God that whatever I will say will be the truth . . .' I had taken my oath.

I had narrated everything I knew about Madanlal, and . . . on 21 January 1948, in the newspaper I had read about the abortive bomb explosion at Gandhiji's prayer meeting and the arrest of Madanlal. Angad Singh had come to me early in the morning and immediately we decided to inform Sardar Patel who had been in Bombay. Unfortunately, we could not reach him as he had by then left for the airport. I had tried to contact S K Patil, President, Bombay Provincial Congress Committee but I was told that he had also accompanied Sardar Patel. I had then contacted B G Kher, Premier of Bombay.

Court: 'Did you actually meet him?'
I: 'Yes, Sir. I had an appointment at 4.00 pm at the Secretariat. I met both B G Kher and Morarji Desai, and apprised them of everything that I knew of the conspiracy.'

Daphtary insisted on his point that my epoch-making evidence was extremely cardinal as regards the murder case. Daphtary made attempts to justify his contention that my deposition was in no way a false concoction, and there were adequate evidence and corroboration that affirmed my point. Daphtary held that Prof Jain was a respectable man of high academic qualifications, and his evidence was essentially independent of Badge's deposition.

Daphtary then referred to my statement that Madanlal K Pahwa, originally a refugee from Punjab, had bragged to Prof Jain about their conspiracy to assassinate Mahatma Gandhi before the murder was actually committed. About Madanlal and his erratic deposition, Daphtary said that he had suffered a great deal in Pakistan and that had made him reckless in words and in action. He further viewed that this man's weird mentality had actually been fruitfully exploited by all the others belonging to the inimical consortium who had found him *reckless* and *readily willing* to join them in their violent errand.

As for the prime question as to why Madanlal had told Prof Jain—a figure who was in no way involved in their vile business—about their plot, Daphtary repeated his already stated point that Madanlal as a man was of such a temperament that before embarking upon the mission he would boast about it, and in this case in a casual tête-a-tête he would have preferred to tell Prof Jain that they were going on such a mission. Madanlal would have informed him of the plot just to boast of himself.

When it was suggested that Prof Jain's *story about the conspiracy* could possibly be a mere fabrication after he had gone through the newspaper of 21 January 1948 with the sole intention to be in the limelight by getting involved in the case, Daphtary said that in no paper of 21 January 1948, it was reported that there was a conspiracy to kill Mahatma Gandhi. Daphtary also dealt with the other suggestion made by the accused that Prof Jain had concocted the *entire story* about the conspiracy to kill Mahatma Gandhi for he had apprehended that he himself might get caught in the telescope of suspicion by denying to pay any attention to such a 'weird' idea which was in no way worthy of consideration.

Daphtary concluded that, 'In that case it would only be a far-fetched idea to expect an innocent man like Prof J C Jain to apprehend that he might get involved in the case.' Had it been the case of Dada Maharaj and Dixit Maharaj, people who were actually dealing in arms and ammunition, such a suggestion could have a great deal of plausibility, but 'nobody can believe in the case of Prof Jain who is a man of high academic qualifications.'

Daphtary continued that the other part of the event—Madanlal's exposé of the conspiracy—was quite natural. It could have been that Madanlal must have thought of bragging to Prof Jain in a moment of utmost complacency about his going to be something *glorious* by killing Mahatma Gandhi. Hence, Daphtary said, there was no reason the court should not have faith in the credibility of Prof Jain's evidence. In his formal statement, Prof Jain had admitted that he had not taken Madanlal's *boastful* account of the conspiracy seriously. No sooner had Prof Jain read the news of the bomb-explosion in the newspapers than he had decided not to leave any stone unturned and immediately did he attempt to contact Sardar Patel. When he could not reach him – yet another luckless turn about in his noble effort—Jain had straightaway met the Premier and the Home Minister of Bombay, and told them 'everything' he had from Madanlal. Daphtary exhorted saying that 'Prof Jain's statement must be considered systematic and believable.'

Daphtary admitted that Prof Jain had, nevertheless, kept some information to himself. During the cross-examination, Jain had said that he had not told the Magistrate about the assault on Rao Saheb Patwardhan by Madanlal. He had also kept secret all that he knew about Savarkar's prime role in the conspiracy. He had not told the Magistrate that Savarkar had sent for Madanlal, had a two hour talk with him and had asked him to proceed according to their scheme. When Jain's act of keeping certain facts secret was questioned, Daphtary clarified it saying that 'All these [little] things were not considered necessary because the substance of the statement that was really confined to the material thing, the existence of a conspiracy, was placed before the Magistrate.' In other words, Jain had told the Magistrate only the important portion of Madanlal's statement.

Jain had previously made a statement on what he had told Angad Singh the very next day after Madanlal had boisterously revealed their *glorious* scheme to him. Daphtary also pointed out that Angad Singh's own deposition was enough corroboration in itself.

❦

Morarji in witness box

My statements in the court caused rancorous furore in Bombay. When I returned home, people came to see me with curiosity, and general resentment was fast mounting up against the local administration for not granting the due importance of what I had informed well in advance of the tragedy. Although declared banned, the members of the RSS on the other hand squatted in Shivaji Park in front of my house or assembled on the terraces of the adjoining buildings pointing at me.

On 18 August 1948, *Dainik Viswamitra*, the Hindi daily in Bombay, carried the lead news as under:

> The Home Minister Mr Morarji Desai will be going to Delhi in a few days, where he will give evidence before the Magistrate, Shri Atma Charan, in Mahatma Gandhi Murder Case. On Tuesday there was a talk in the Secretariat that Prof Jain of Ruia College has *implicated the Home Minister without any reason* (author's italics). A spokesman of the Bombay Government stated that lawfully it was improper for the Home Minister to give evidence at Delhi, nevertheless, Mr Morarji Desai would definitely go to Delhi with a view to remove the misunderstanding of the people. Mr Desai has been served with summons.

Morarji Desai deposed before the court and the evidences ran as under:

> On getting this (Prof Jain's) information, I sent for the Officer-in-Charge of Intelligence, Mr Nagarwala.

He could not come immediately as he was busy elsewhere. But the same night I was to go to Ahmedabad and so I asked him to see me at the railway station. Mr Nagarwala saw me at the station. I told him the whole story as narrated by Prof Jain and asked him to take necessary action.'

During the court proceedings, various questions were put to Morarji Desai:
'Did you find out the antecedents of Prof Jain?'
'No, I did not.'
'Did you ask Mr Nagarwala to keep a watch over Prof Jain?'
'I did not.'
'Do you know how many interviews Prof Jain had with Mr Nagarwala after he was put in contact with him?'
'I do not know.'
'Will you tell the court reasons for your believing the story of Prof Jain?'
'I have long experience of judging stories because I was a Magistrate for about 11 years. The frankness with which Prof Jain narrated me the story caused me to believe he was telling the truth. When Prof Jain was telling me the story, my experience as a Magistrate had automatically come into operation.'

Desai's unsolicited credential was no consolation since I could not save Bapu. I had passed over all the relevant information and 'had slightest keenness been shown in the investigation of the case at that stage', Atma Charan, the Judge had observed, 'the tragedy probably could have been avoided'.

Prosecution examines Madanlal

Daphtary focused on the events and actions that did obviously and unfalteringly run against Madanlal K Pahwa's plea of [partial] innocence; or, at least his himself being a victim of the conspiracy. Daphtary in his deliberation held that Madanlal himself had admitted his presence in Delhi on 20 January 1948, and that he himself had exploded the gun cotton-slab. Madanlal had claimed that his role in the conspiracy against Mahatma Gandhi was a case of mere capitulation: he 'had' to agree to take part in it without his own moral consent.

According to Madanlal, despite his connivance, it was his utmost wish to avoid his part in such a heinous intrigue. To effect his relief and breakout of the conspiratorial circle even after getting arms and ammunition, he had decided to explode one gun cotton-slab at Mahatma Gandhi's prayer ground and thus courted arrest. His sole point was that in such a circumstance he would have seen Mahatma Gandhi in person to inform him of the sufferings of the Hindu refugees.

Daphtary annulled such a plea stating that what Madanlal claimed to be true was, indeed, 'sheer absurdity' for no sane man would volunteer to court arrest after exploding such a dangerous thing. Moreover, if Madanlal really had the pious intention to meet 'Gandhiji' at his prayer ground to convey his message, he could have made a demonstration and shouted some slogans as he had done on a previous occasion in front of Pandit Nehru, the Prime Minister. Daphtary ardently added, 'I am sure in that case Mahatma Gandhi would have given him a better hearing.'

Shankar's plea

Shankar Kistaiya, the servant of the arms dealer Digambar Badge, was basically arraigned by Daphtary on the charge of having an entire knowledge of the conspirators, their conspiracy, and thus passively colluding with the confederates. Daphtary submitted that Shankar had admitted his presence in Delhi on 19 and 20 January 1948; he had also admitted having met Narayan D Apte, Vishnu R Karkare, Madanlal K Pahwa, Digambar R Badge, Gopal V Godse and Nathuram V Godse in the Marina Hotel in the afternoon of 20 January 1948, and also having gone to the Birla House in the evening in company with Narayan D Apte, Gopal V Godse and Digambar R Badge. Shankar did not, however, admit that he had been made aware of the object of their going to the Birla House by Badge prior to their actual meeting. Daphtary thereupon adjudicated that Shankar had practically corroborated Badge; that the presence of Shankar at Marina Hotel at the time of the distribution of arms and ammunition, subsequent presence in the jungle behind the Hindu Mahasabha Bhawan, and his visit to the Birla House clearly indicated that he did surely know the object.

Gopal nailed

As for the case against Gopal V Godse, Daphtary held that since Gopal could not provide sufficient and conclusive evidence to prove his statement that he was not in Delhi on 19 and 20 January 1948, and instead he was in his village Uksan, his plea would not hold good in the circumstances and could only be construed as a mere creation of his fancy; hence, as false as a story.

~

Savarkar's Trial

It was 20 November 1948 on which day the examination of Vinayak Damodar Savarkar was scheduled, and expectedly the attention from all quarters was aimed at the Special Court situated at the Red Fort, Delhi.

With the case against Vinayak D Savarkar, the ex-president of the Hindu Mahasabha, Daphtary cited sufficiently ample evidence to establish his unflinching association with Narayan D Apte, Nathuram V Godse and all other delinquents who were on remand.

First, Daphtary presented evidence showing that Nathuram V Godse and Narayan D Apte had gone to Savarkar Sadan sometime in the evening of 14 January 1948, and that later again Apte, Godse, and Badge had visited Savarkar Sadan. On their return visit, they had a bag containing arms and explosives.

Secondly, the Prosecution Counsel referred to Prof Jain's evidence that Savarkar had patted Madanlal and praised him to the skies on hearing his exploits at Ahmednagar.

Thirdly, Daphtary referred to the evidence that on 15 January 1948 Apte had told Badge and others that Savarkar had decided that Mahatma Gandhi, Pandit Jawaharlal Nehru and Suhrawardy 'should be finished off' (i.e. killed or assassinated), thereupon entrusted such a 'detestable responsibility' with them all.

Fourthly, Daphtary postulated that Savarkar was most certainly a close associate of the delinquents by referring to the evidences that on 17 January 1948 Nathuram V Godse had suggested that they should go to have the last 'darshan' (i.e. visit) of Savarkar, and, when they had come out of Savarkar Sadan, Savarkar had wished that they be successful.

Fifthly, Daphtary reminded Itapa Kotian's (the taxi-driver) deposition stating that he had heard Apte saying that Savarkar had predicted that 'Gandhiji's 100 years are over'.

Sixthly, the Prosecution had also led evidence to the effect that a personal telephone call had been booked from the Hindu Mahasabha Bhawan, Delhi in favour of the Secretary of Savarkar.

Atma Charan, the Special Judge, called for Accused No 7, Vinayak Damodar Savarkar, Hindu, aged 66, and his statement was recorded u/s 364 of the Cr P C.

Q. You have heard the entire evidence produced on behalf of the prosecution against you. What have you to say?

A. I have filed my written statement.

Q. It is in evidence as below:

About 2-3 days after the end of the first week of January 1948 Madanlal told Dr J C Jain that when you heard of his (Madanlal's) exploits at Ahmednagar you sent for him, had a long talk with him for about two hours, patted him on his back and said 'carry on'.

Would you like to suggest anything?

A. This is all false.

Q. It is in evidence as below:

On 14 January at about 7.30 pm Miss Shanta B
Modak dropped Nathuram Godse and Apte opposite
to your house.

Would you like to suggest anything?

A. I know nothing about it.

Q. It is in evidence as below:

On 14 January 1948 at about 9.00 pm Nathuram
Godse and Apte went to your house with a bag said
to be containing explosives. They then left your house
shortly thereafter with the bag.

Would you like to suggest anything?

A. This is all false.

Q. It is in evidence as below:

On 15 January 1948 in the compound of the house
of Dixitji Maharaj, Apte in the presence of Nathuram
Godse, told Badge that you had decided that
Mahatma Gandhi, Jawaharlal Nehru and Suhawardy
should be 'finished' and had entrusted that work to
them.

Would you like to suggest anything?

A. This is all false.

Q. It is in evidence as below:

On 17 January 1948 Nathuram Godse, Apte and
Badge went to your house. Nathuram Godse and
Apte went upstairs, and Badge waited in the room
on the ground floor. Nathuram Godse and Apte
then came down after 5-10 minutes. They were
followed immediately by you. You said 'Yashasvi
Houn Ya.'

Would you like to suggest anything?

A. This is altogether false.

Q. It is in evidence as below:

Apte on return from your house told those in the taxi that you had predicted that Gandhiji's 100 years were over. Apte then said that there was no doubt that their work would be successfully finished.

Would you like to suggest anything?

A. I did not say any such thing to anyone at any time. I cannot say what Apte said on his own behalf to anyone.

Q. It is in evidence as below:

On 19 January 1948 at about 9.20 am a telephonic call was booked for Damle or Kasar from Delhi 8024 to Bombay 60201. Damle is your Secretary and Kasar your Body-Guard. Bombay 60201 is your telephone number at Savarkar-Sadan.

Would you like to suggest anything?

A. I know nothing about the booking of the telephonic call. Damle is my Secretary and Kasar my Body-Guard. The call, if so booked, was booked not in their official capacity but in their personal capacity. Bombay 60201 is the telephone number of my residence.

Q. It is in evidence as below:

On 31 January 1948 a search was made at your house and a large volume of correspondence was taken possession of by the Police. Exhibits P 87, P 88 and P 277, P 302 are said to be part of the correspondence so seized from your possession. Exhibits P 87 and P 88 bear the signatures of Badge. Exhibits P 277 and P 302 bear the signatures of Nathuram Godse and/or Apte or your signature or signatures on your behalf.

Would you like to suggest anything?

A. Yes, it is so.

Q. It is in evidence as below:

You are said to have been well acquainted with Nathuram Godse, Apte, Karkare, Madanlal, Parchure and Badge prior to 17 January 1948.

Would you like to suggest anything?

A. I was well acquainted with Nathuram Godse and Apte in their capacity as workers of the Hindu Mahasabha. I had heard of the names of Karkare, Parchure and Badge, but did not know them personally. I did not at all know Madanlal and had not even heard of his name.

Q. You have heard the entire evidence produced on behalf of the prosecution against you.

Would you like to say or suggest anything more before the Court?

A. No. I have already filed my written statement.

Q. Do you want to adduce evidence in defence?

A. No. I do not want to adduce evidence in defence.

༺❀༻

Approver Badge's deposition facilitates

In the Gandhi Murder Trial, the prosecution case was largely based on the approver, Digambar Badge's deposition. Daphtary urged upon the court to rely on Digambar R Badge's sworn evidence and on whatever he had stated during the prosecution. Daphtary submitted that the 'examination-in-chief' or 'direct-examination' of Badge alone ran into 23 pages. It was a proof enough to believe Badge's evidence because if he were never a 'party-to-the-conspiracy', and if he had never been, directly or indirectly, involved in the assassination, he would never have gone into-either verifiable or already proven-details. On the contrary, he remembered all the events with such meticulousness, was sufficient proof of his being an active help to all the others involved in the murder case. Daphtary retorted, 'Is it not impossible for an innocent man to remember, or, perhaps, concoct, a well thought out story which never existed, pages after pages?' Digambar's assertion was lucid and persuasively convincing. Furthermore, Daphtary added, 'Badge gave his evidence clearly and confidently.'

On being asked by Atma Charan, the Special Judge, if Badge's evidence was corroborated by any other evidence intrinsically related in this case, Daphtary posited that there had been cases in which approver's evidence was accepted without corroboration. In the present case corroboration was also there, and whether the corroboration was sufficient or not, the court had to assess the value of the approver's deposition.

More evidence

At first, Daphtary referred to the evidence of Miss Shanta Modak who had stated that she had dropped Nathuram V Godse and Narayan D Apte in front of Savarkar Sadan and had seen them proceeding towards Savarkar Sadan. Mehar Singh, the forest guard, had indentified Gopal V Godse as the person with whom he had a talk in the jungle behind Hindu Mahasabha Bhawan on 20 January 1948.

Surjit Singh, a taxi driver, had deposed that on 20 January 1948, at about 4.15 pm he had taken in his taxi, a green Chevrolet PBF 671, four persons from the taxi stand in front of the Regal Cinema to the Birla House. Surjit Singh had indentified Digambar R Badge, his servant Shankar Kistaiya, Narayan D Apte, and Gopal V Godse as those persons who had travelled in his taxi. Surjit Singh had further stated that Apte had directed him to park the taxi at a particular place. The taxi driver had also stated that the person who sat in the front seat did not come in his taxi on the return journey, but another person (pointing towards Nathuram Godse) had come in his place. He had also stated that after the explosion, the occupants of his taxi came to him and had hurriedly told him 'start the car, start the car.'

Dixit Maharaj, in his evidence, had stated that Godse, Apte, and Badge had come to see him on 15 January 1948 in the morning. They had asked his servant Narain to bring out the bag which was left by them on the previous day. The bag was brought out and the explosives were taken out of it. Dixit Maharaj had also stated that Apte and Godse needed a revolver, and they had demanded one from him.

Itapa Kotian, a taxi driver of Bombay, had deposed that he had taken in his taxi Apte, Godse and Badge to various places from 7.15 am to 1.30 pm on 17 January 1948. He had also identified Afzalpurkar, Kale, and Patankar, the three persons who had appeared as witnesses. Kotian's statement was also supported by Afzalpurkar and Kale who had admitted that Apte, Godse, and Badge did visit them on 17 January 1948, and they had given Rs 100 and Rs 1,000 respectively to the inimical trio.

Dada Maharaj had corroborated Badge regarding the flight of Apte and Godse on 17 January 1948 from

Bombay to Delhi. He had also said in his evidence that when he proceeded to Pandharpur, a man coming from Apte had told him that Apte wanted to see him on his way back at Poona. Daphtary presumed that the man sent by Apte was Karkare. Dada Maharaj had also had a conversation with Godse and Apte in which Dada Maharaj had said that they were merely talking and doing nothing. Apte had replied that Dada Maharaj would know when something was done. If, what they had in mind was a peaceful and innocent demonstration to be staged at the prayer-meeting of Mahatma Gandhi, as Daphtary observed, that was not something which was to be shown to Dada Maharaj. Their association with Dada Maharaj was regarding the blowing up of trains, supplying of explosives and such material which would induce in Dada Maharaj a reasonable anticipation of something very grand being done.

In his deliberation with regard to Dr Parchure, Daphtary submitted before the Special Judge, Atma Charan that the concerned person, the delinquent in the dock, had made a confession accepting the fact that he knew two persons who had come to him at Gwalior on 27 January 1948 and they had overtly made their intention clear that they were going to Delhi to perpetrate a murder. He had confessed that they required a revolver for that purpose, and thus Daphtary deduced from such a confession that it was indeed a clear admission of the offence of having definite communication with Narayan D Apte and Nathuram V Godse regarding the assassination and hence a clear clue to Dr Parchure's playing a crucial part as a conspirator. In addition to this, the evidence of Madhukar Kale and Khire bore out the fact that Nathuram V Godse and

Narayan D Apte did go to Gwalior on 27 January 1948 to procure a revolver. Daphtary soon brought in the point relating to the nationality of Dr Parchure and presented records—as his evidence to justify his contention—to show that being Sadashiv Gopal Parchure's son, and being born and educated in Poona, Dr Parchure was also a British subject, although he did serve in Gwalior State.

Daphtary then turned his attention to Amchekar's travelling with Karkare and Madanlal from Bombay to Delhi. All of them had alighted at the Delhi on 17 January 1948 and stayed together in the Sharif Hotel. In his revelatory deposition, Amchekar specified that when he had entered his room in the Sharif Hotel on 19 January 1948, he had found Karkare and Madanlal with another person. Amchekar had distinctly recounted that Madanlal was sitting on a cot and Karkare and the stranger were conversing with each other.

Next, Daphtary referred to Sulochana Devi's evidence in which she said that she had seen Madanlal placing a bomb at the prayer-meeting or 20 January 1948 and setting it alight. The witness had also identified Digambar R Badge, Nathuram V Godse, and Narayan D Apte, who were present in the Birla House that day.

Bhur Singh, a watchman of the Birla House, had also identified Nathuram Godse, Apte, Karkare, Madanlal, Gopal Godse, and Badge whom he had seen at the Birla House before the explosion of the gun-cotton slab on 20 January 1948. The watchman had also testified the recovery of a hand-grenade and the coat from Madanlal who had, during the cross-examination, denied saying that the coat did not belong to him. Sardar Dasondha Singh, the Inspector of Police, and Mr Sawhny, the

Magistrate had, however, affirmed that the coat that was exhibited actually belonged to Madanlal, and that it was the same coat that he wore at the time of his arrest on 20 January 1948. The trousers corresponding to this coat were found from the trunk of Apte. Dabke, a tailor of Poona, had testified that he knew Apte for the last six or seven years and he himself had stitched both the trousers and the coat for Apte.

Moving on to Chamanlal Grover's evidence, the Chief Prosecution Counsel said that Grover had testified the recovery of certain articles from the jungle behind the Hindu Mahasabha Bhawan. Digambar Badge's servant Shankar Kistaiya had pointed out in the jungle, on 11 February 1948, in the presence of Grover, among other things, two hand-grenades which had been, as Daphtary pointed out, taken to the prayer-ground on 20 January 1948 by Badge and Shankar. This view was corroborated by Badge's identification of 'cross-mark with a red pencil' on these hand-grenades.

Godbole and Kale had confirmed that Gopal V Godse had given a revolver to Godbole somewhere about 22-23 January 1948. Godbole had kept it with him till 30 January 1948, and subsequently he had given it to Kale for disposal. Daphtary pointed out that was one of the revolvers which had been brought to Delhi on 20 January 1948 and taken back.

Dealing with the evidence of the witnesses from Marina Hotel, Daphtary quoted the evidence of Ramchand, a receptionist of the Marina Hotel, who had stated that Apte and Nathuram Godse had stayed in Room no 40 of Marina Hotel under the assumed names of 'S Deshpande' and 'M Deshpande'. Nain Singh, a bearer of Marina Hotel, had stated that on 20 January

1948, at about tea-time first he had served tea to the two occupants of Room no 40 and then he was asked to serve three extra cups of tea. He recounted that five cups in all were served. According to Kaleram, Nathuram Godse did not ask even for the clothes which had been given for washing while leaving the hotel on 20 January 1948. Another bearer of Marina Hotel had served whisky to Karkare in Room no 40. According to the co-manager of the hotel, Madanlal led a police party to Room no 40 of Marina Hotel on 20 January 1948 and had told the police that his friends had been staying there.

Om Prakash of Frontier Hotel, Delhi, had stated in his evidence that 'Rajagopalan'—whom he later identified as Gopal Godse and 'G Joshi' whom he identified as Karkare—had stayed in the Frontier Hotel on 20 January 1948. Similarly from the evidence of Sundarilal, Harikrishna, and Janu Jyoti, it was established that Narayan D Apte, Nathuram V Godse, and Vishnu R Karkare were in Delhi on 29 and 30 January 1948.

Special Judge delivers his judgement

After hearing the arguments of both the sides, Atma Charan, the Special Judge delivered his judgment in the Red Fort, Delhi on 10 February 1949, as follows:

Nathuram Godse intentionally and knowingly caused the death of Mahatma Gandhi on 30 January 1948. The act of Nathuram Godse in committing the murder of Mahatma Gandhi was a deliberate and a calculated one. No extenuating circumstances have been pointed, nor could have been pointed out on his behalf. The only sentence, in the circumstances, that could be passed on him, under Section 302 of the Indian Penal Code, is the sentence of death.

The act of Apte in abetting the offence of the murder of Mahatma Gandhi is in no way less heinous. Throughout he took the lead at each stage of the crime and at the most crucial moment either just ran away or just absented himself from the scene of the crime. Had it not been for his brain work, the murder of Mahatma Gandhi probably would never have been committed. The only sentence, in the circumstances, that could be passed on him, under Section 109 of the Indian Penal Code, read with Section 302 of the Code, is the sentence of death.

So far as Karkare, Gopal Godse and Parchure are concerned, it would, in my opinion, meet the ends of justice if they are sentenced each to undergo transportation for life, under Section 109 of the Indian Penal Code, read with Section 302 of the Code. This is the minimum sentence awardable under Section 109 of the Indian Penal Code, read with Section 302 of the Code.

Now the question is what sentences should be awarded to Madanlal and Shankar Kistaiya, under Sections 120(B) and 115 of the Indian Penal Code, read with Section 302 of the Code? It would, in my opinion, meet the ends of justice if they are sentenced each to undergo transportation for life under Section 302 of the Code. This is the minimum sentence awardable under Section 120(B) of the Indian Penal Code, read with Section 302 of the Code. There is nothing on the record of the case to show as to why a lenient view at all be taken in regard to the offence punishable under Section 115 of the Indian Penal Code, read with Section 302 of the Code. Madanlal and Shankar Kistaiya, in the circumstances, should be sentenced each to undergo seven years' rigorous imprisonment, under Section 115 of the Indian Penal Code, read with Section 302 of the Code.

Shankar Kistaiya is the servant of Badge. Whatever he did, he did more or less in obedience to the orders of his master. Unless it was for Badge he would never have been approached by the other accused to join the conspiracy. Shankar Kistaiya, in the circumstances, certainly deserves some leniency. I would accordingly recommend that his sentence for transportation for life, under Section 120(B) of the Indian Penal Code, read with Section 302 of the Code, may be commuted to seven years' rigorous imprisonment under Section 401 and 402 of the Code of Criminal Procedure.

It would, in my opinion, meet the ends of justice if Nathuram Godse and Apte are sentenced each to undergo two years rigorous imprisonment, under Section 19(C) of the Indian Arms Act, or, in the alternative, under Section 114 of the Indian Penal Code, read with Section 19(C) of the Indian Arms Act, if Nathuram Godse is sentenced to undergo two years' rigorous imprisonment under Section 19(F) of the Indian Arms Act and if Apte and Karkare are sentenced each to undergo two years' rigorous imprisonment under Section 114 of the Indian Penal Code, read with Section 19 (F) of the Indian Arms Act.

It would, in my opinion, meet the ends of justice if Nathuram Godse, Apte, Karkare, Madanlal, Shankar Kistaiya and Gopal Godse are sentenced each to undergo three years' rigorous imprisonment under Section 5 of the Explosive Substances Act, or, in the alternative, under Section 5 of the Explosive Substances Act, read with

Section 6 of the Act, five years' rigorous imprisonment under Section 4(B) of the Explosive Substances Act, read with Section 6 of the Act; if Nathuram Godse, Apte, Karkare, Shankar Kistaiya, Gopal Godse are sentenced each to undergo seven years' rigorous imprisonment, under Section 8 of the Explosive Substances Act, read with Section 6 of the Act; if Madanlal is sentenced to undergo ten years' rigorous imprisonment under Section 8 of the Explosive Substances Act.

Digamber R Badge was given pardon and was released from custody. Badge was first produced before the Court on 27 May 1948. He had no counsel, and was asked if he wanted to engage one at the expense of the Crown. He refused the offer but wanted to make a true statement of the facts. His statement was not recorded by the Court at that stage. He had been interrogated twice by J D Nagarwala. Ordinance XIV of 1948 was passed by the Central Government on 14 June 1948, empowering courts constituted under Section 10 and 11 of the Bombay Public Security Measures Act, as extended to the province of Delhi, to tender a pardon to an accused. The counsel for the prosecution put in an application before the Court on 17 June 1948 seeking pardon for Badge. He was examined in due course and was tendered a pardon by the Court on 21 June 1948.

It has been argued on behalf of the defence that the proceedings with regard to the tender of pardon were invalid, as those proceedings had been conducted without notice to the accused and in their absence. The contention carries no weight whatsoever, as the granting of pardon is a matter between the approver and the Court. There is no provision in law that notice must be given to the other accused or that the other accused must be heard on an application for such grant.

It has been argued on behalf of the defence that the Court had no power to tender a pardon to an accused, as the case had not been received after commitment, as required under Section 338 of the Code of Criminal Procedure. Section 13(3) of the Bombay Public Security Measures Act, as extended to the province of Delhi, clearly lays down that in matters not within the scope of subsections (1) and (2), the provisions of the Code, in so far as they are not inconsistent with the provisions of Sections 10 to 20, shall apply to the proceedings of a Special Judge; and for the purpose of the said provision, the Court of the Special Judge shall be deemed to be a Court of Session. Section 338 of the Code of Criminal Procedure lays down that at any time after commitment, but before any judgment is passed, the Court to which the commitment is made may tender a pardon. The words 'at any time and after commitment' and 'before judgment is passed', refer to the stage at which the Court of Session may tender a pardon to an accused, and in the present case just means that the Special Court may tender a pardon to an accused, but only after it has taken care of the case under Section 13(1) of the Bombay Public Security Measures Act, as extended to the province of Delhi. The matter, however, has now been beyond any doubt by the Ordinance XIV of 1948 and Central Act III of 1948.

It has been contended on behalf of the defence that the approver should have been called first to give his evidence before other witnesses. In the present case, the prosecution first led the evidence in regard to what occurred at Delhi on 20 January 1948 and 30 January 1948. They led the evidence of the approver thereafter. They then led the evidence in regard to what took place at Bombay from 14 to 17 January 1948. No doubt it would have been better if the prosecution had produced the approver first and led the evidence in regard to the incidents in Delhi on 20 January 1948 thereafter. However, there is nothing in law which obliges the prosecution to call witnesses in any particular order. The accused in the present case had been supplied with a summary of evidence of the main prosecution witnesses. There is thus no reason to suppose that the accused have, in any way whatsoever, been prejudiced by not producing the approver first to give his evidence.

It is now practically a rule of law that an approver must be corroborated, both as to the *corpus delicii* and as to the identity of the accused, though corroboration need not be on all the details of the crime, nor is it necessary that the corroborative evidence should itself be sufficient for conviction. The nature and the extent of the corroboration required depend upon and vary with the circumstances of each case, particularly the nature of the offence charged, the character and the antecedents of the approver and the degree of suspicion attaching to the evidence, the circumstances in which the approver makes his statement and his motive to implicate the accused falsely.

The examination and the cross-examination of the approver went on from 20 to 30 July 1948. Badge was cross-examined for nearly a week. There was thus ample opportunity to observe his demeanour and the way in which he gave evidence. He presented his version of the facts in a direct and straightforward manner. He did not evade cross-examination or attempt to evade or fence with any question. It would not have been possible for anyone to have given evidence so unfalteringly, stretching over such a long period and with such particularity with regard to the facts which had not occurred at all. It is difficult to conceive of anyone memorising so long and so detailed a story, if altogether without foundation.

The evidence of the approver may conveniently be divided into three groups: firstly, the evidence that stands fully corroborated, secondly, the evidence that stands generally corroborated and thirdly, the evidence that does not stand corroborated in regard to the identity of a certain accused.

The approver in his evidence says that he dealt in arms, ammunition and explosives and that Karkare and Madanlal, along with two more individuals, came to inspect the explosives at his house on 9 January 1948. He was summoned to the Hindu Rashtra office on 10 January 1948 when he agreed to supply Nathuram Godse and Apte with two gun-cotton slabs and five hand-grenades at the Hindu Mahasabha office at Dadar on 14 January 1948.

It has been argued on behalf of the defence that the individuals who are said to have accompanied Karkare and Madanlal to the house of the approver on 9 January 1948 could at least have been produced in corroboration of the approver's story. The evidence produced on behalf of the prosecution shows that every effort was made to trace them, but in vain. Even if they had appeared as witnesses it is doubtful if their evidence would have amounted to more than that of the accomplices.

The approver in his evidence says that he was asked by Apte in the compound of the temple of Dixitji Maharaj to proceed along with them to Delhi, as it had been decided that Mahatma Gandhi be 'finished'. He agreed. Along with Shankar Kistaiya he proceeded to Delhi and stayed in the Hindu Mahasabha Bhawan with Madanlal and Gopal Godse on 19 and 20 January 1948.

It has been argued on behalf of the defence that at least someone should have been produced from the Hindu Mahasabha Bhawan in corroboration of the approver's story. However, the prosecution could have produced no such person in evidence, in view of their allegations against the Hindu Mahasabha.

The approver in his evidence says that Apte took him, along with Shankar Kistaiya, on 20 January 1948 to Birla House and showed him the prayer platform, the window with trellis-work behind it and the servants' quarters.

It has been argued on behalf of the defence that at least the gate-keeper and some servants living in the quarters should have been produced in corroboration of the approver's story. It is just possible that the gate-keeper and the servants might not have taken any serious notice of the visit of these persons to the Birla House that day. However, it quite stands to reason that Apte would have shown the prayer platform and the surrounding locality to the approver, before proceeding for the intended object to that place. He could not have just asked the approver to enter the place unless he had explained beforehand how the matter stood and what was intended to be done there.

In his evidence, the approver says that on 20 January 1948 in the Marina Hotel they fixed primers to the gun-cotton slabs and detonators to the hand-grenades, discussed the plan and distributed the 'stuff' among themselves. Of course, no direct corroboration evidence to the effect could possibly have been produced on behalf of the prosecution. However, there is an illuminating piece of indirect corroborative evidence to the effect on behalf of the prosecution. The evidence of Nain Singh, as supported by Exhibits P 17 and P 24, goes to show that three extra teas had been ordered and supplied that day in Room no 40.

It is a well-known principle in the estimation of evidence that the earlier events may be construed in the light of the subsequent ones. The approver's story, as given above, fits in fully with the events that took place subsequently and stands corroborated otherwise by independent evidence. There is thus no reason as to why reliance be not placed on the approver's evidence that stands generally corroborated.

The approver in his evidence states that on 14 January 1948 Nathuram Godse and Apte took him from the Hindu Mahasabha office at Dadar to Savarkar Sadan, saying that arrangements will have to be made for keeping the 'stuff'. He had the bag containing the 'stuff' with him; Nathuram Godse and Apte then went inside, leaving him standing outside Savarkar Sadan. Nathuram Godse and Apte came back 5 to 10 minutes later with the bag containing the 'stuff'.

The approver then says that on 15 January 1948 in the compound of the temple of Dixitji Maharaj, Apte told him that Savarkar had decided that Gandhiji should be 'finished' and had entrusted that work to them. The approver then says that on 17 January 1948 Nathuram Godse suggested that they should all go and have the last darshan of Savarkar and they proceeded to Savarkar

Sadan. Apte asked him to wait in the room on the ground floor and came down after 5 to 10 minutes. They were immediately followed by Savarkar, who addressed Nathuram Godse and Apte saying *'Yashasvi Houn Ya'* (Be successful and come).

Badge said that from Savarkar Sadan Savarkar had predicted *'Tatyaraovani ase bhavishya kele ahe ki Gandhijichi shabhar varshe bharali—ata apale kam nischite honar, yat kahi sanshaya nahi'* (Gandhiji's 100 years were over, there was no doubt that our work would be successfully finished).

The accused were informed that if they wished to appeal against the order they could do so within 15 days.

Savarkar's acquittal

In the judgement of the Special Court, Savarkar was not found guilty of the offence, as specified in the charge, and was acquitted.

The prosecution case against Savarkar appeared to rest just on the evidence of the approver and the approver alone. The contention on behalf of the prosecution is that part of the approver's story as against Savarkar to certain extent stands corroborated by the evidence of Miss Shantibai B Modak and Itapa Kotian.

No doubt there was the evidence of Miss Shantibai B Modak that Nathuram Godse and Apte got down in front of Savarkar Sadan on 14 January 1948. The evidence to the effect, however, in no way established that Nathuram Godse and Apte had alighted in front of Savarkar Sadan to visit Savarkar. The evidence on record in the case showed that not only Savarkar, but A S Bhide and Gajanan Damle also resided in Savarkar Sadan. No doubt there was also the evidence of Itapa Kotian that

Nathuram Godse, Apte and the approver got down at Shivaji Park on 17 January 1948. But the evidence to the effect, however, was no corroboration of the approver's story in regard to what the approver said that he heard Savarkar saying to Nathuram Godse and Apte. The approver in his evidence held that he had just heard Savarkar saying to Nathuram Godse and Apte *'Yashasvi Houn Ya'*.

Nothing on record would show as to what conversation had taken place just prior to that on the first floor between Nathuram Godse, Apte and Savarkar. Accordingly, there was no reason to suppose that the remark said to have been addressed by Savarkar to Nathuram Godse and Apte in the presence of the approver was in reference to the assassination plot against Mahatma Gandhi.

Atma Charan held that it would be unsafe to base any conclusion on the approver's story given above as against Savarkar.

Finally, passing severe strictures against the Delhi and Bombay Police, the Special Judge remarked: 'I may bring to the notice of the Central Government the slackness of the police in the investigation of the case during the period between 20 and 30 January 1948. The Delhi Police had obtained a detailed statement from Madanlal soon after his arrest on 20 January 1948. The Bombay Police had also been reported the statement of Dr J C Jain that he made to the Honourable Morarji Desai on 21 January 1948. The Delhi police and the Bombay police had contacted each other soon after these statements had been made. Yet the police miserably failed to derive any advantage from these two statements. Had the slightest keenness being shown in the investigations of the case at the stage, the tragedy probably could have been averted.'

Vinayak Damodar Savarkar's being acquitted of the charge of the conspiracy to murder Gandhi was sound in law because the approver, Digambar Badge's evidences, though trustworthy otherwise, lacked independent corroboration; a common flaw in conspiracy cases notwithstanding the Judge Atma Charan accepted Badge as a truthful witness.

> 'He gave his version of the facts in a direct and straight-forward manner. He did not evade cross-examination or attempt to evade or fence with any question.'

A probe into the court affairs during Savarkar's trial would, however, enable one to reasonably conclude that Savarkar's version was indeed far away from his conspiratorial proximity to the assassin Godse and his accomplice Apte.

> 'Pandit Godse and Narayan Apte got themselves introduced to me as Hindu Mahasabha workers at Nagar and Poona and later on came to be personally acquainted with me.'

Gopal Godse's revelations as available in his Marathi book *Gandhi Hatya, Ani Me* ('Gandhi's Murder and I'), published in 1967 after Savarkar's death, claimed to be much more than *acquaintance*. Once Savarkar was set free in 1937, 'Nathuram started going about with Veer Savarkar everywhere.' As it had surfaced later, a close bond was shared between Savarkar and Godse, and comparing the relationship with that of 'guru' and 'shishya' would not be an understatement. In an undated letter, possibly written in March 1946 referring to the second anniversary of 'Agrani' (founded on 28 March 1944), Godse was appreciative of the benevolence shown by his mentor Savarkar. 'You have given me a large sum of Rs 15,000 for the purpose', Godse had written and this betrayed 'how close this cause is to your heart'. A detailed account of *Agrani* stretched itself to survive in the face of newsprint shortages, a ban, and a lack of funds was submitted to Savarkar. Godse had asked his 'guru' for a further 'loan' of Rs 10,000, promising to repay the amount at an interest of 3 per cent a month. He had also assured Savarkar that *Agrani* was the only newspaper in Maharashtra that would work towards disseminating Savarkar's thought, 'In Maharashtra today, the only paper that works towards disseminating your ideas is this, and your contribution of Rs 15,000 is testimony of your association with it. This is common knowledge and requires little proof. These matters, and some other matters need to be discussed with you in person,' Godse had continued, and proposed to meet Savarkar at Walchandnagar with Apte during the following week. Godse had concluded, 'Whether your answer is yes or no, do not get angry with your shishya or hold it against him. This is my entreaty to you.'

Appeal Court verdict

A full bench of the East Punjab High Court, Simla, consisting of Justice Bhandari, Justice Achhruram and Justice Khosla, while delivering their judgment on 21 June 1948 in the appeal preferred by Nathuram Godse and six others in the Gandhi Murder Case against the order of Atma Charan, Judge of the Special Court, unanimously allowed the appeals of Sadashiv Parchure of Gwalior and Shankar Kistaiya, the servant of the approver Badge, and acquitted them of all the charges.

The appeals of the remaining convicts—Nathuram Godse, Narayan Apte, Vishnu R Karkare, Madanlal Pahwa and Gopal Godse—were rejected. Nathuram Godse and Apte were sentenced to death for murder of Mahatma Gandhi and the conspiracy to murder, and the remaining three accused were given the sentence of transportation for life.

Their lordship, however, unanimously recommended that in the case of Gopal Godse, brother of Nathuram Godse, the power of clemency which vested in the Crown should be exercised in his favour.

Justice Bhandari and Justice Khosla disagreed with the recommendation of Justice Achhruram to commend the case of Madanlal to the Government for consideration and the desirability of commuting the sentence of transportation for life passed on him.

Justice Bhandari, the Presiding Judge, with whom the other Judges concurred in the conclusions of his judgement, observed,

'I am of the opinion that the prosecution have failed to bring the charges home to Parchure beyond reasonable doubt. I would accept the appeal preferred by him, set aside the order of the learned Special Judge and direct that he be set at liberty.'

Discussing the case of Shankar Kistaiya, the Judge remarked: 'The case of Shankar is also open to doubt that he was not a member of the conspiracy which was formed to take the life of Mahatma Gandhi. In addition to his conviction upon a conspiracy to murder, he was convicted for contravention of the provisions of the Indian Arms Act and the Indian Explosives Act.'

'His employer Badge was dealing extensively in arms and explosives and it is probable that this prisoner has committed offences in connection with the two said acts. Unfortunately, for the ends of justice, no independent evidence has been produced in corroboration of the testimony of Badge that Shankar was, in fact, guilty of the said offences. I am accordingly of the opinion that although there is a very strong suspicion that he offended against the provisions of the appropriate enactments, no action can be taken against him. I would accordingly accept the appeal preferred by Shankar and acquit him of all the charges of which he has been convicted.'

Dealing with the other cases the learned Judge remarked, 'Nathuram and Apte were so highly dissatisfied with the policy which was being pursued by Mahatma Gandhi that they started a newspaper for counter-acting the said policy. They staged peaceful demonstrations with the object of dissuading Mahatma Gandhi from pursuing a course of action which, according to them, was suicidal to the interests of this country. When they found that neither written nor verbal protests could influence Mahatma Gandhi to alter his life-long policy, they decided to remove this apostle of non-violence by violent methods. The murder was pre-meditated, cold-blooded and cruel, and the only punishment that could be awarded to these two prisoners for the commission of so heinous a crime is that of death.'

Karkare and Madanlal had also been found guilty under Section 120(B)/302 of the Indian Penal Code and of certain other sections of certain other provisions of law and had been sentenced to transportation for life.

Karkare was imbued with the same ideas as Nathuram and Apte, but the interest evinced by him in connection with this conspiracy was considerably less than that of his more determined associates. They found a useful tool in the person of Madanlal and gave him an important part in the incident which was to take place at Birla House on 20 January 1948. He lighted a gun-cotton slab with the object of creating an explosion and, if the other conspirators had played the parts assigned to them, Mahatma Gandhi's life would have been terminated on 20 January 1948.

Madanlal had taken an active, though a secondary part in carrying out the nefarious designs of Nathuram, Apte and Karkare, but the fact that he actually set light to the gun-cotton slab showed that the enormity of the crime committed by him was no less than that of the crime committed by Karkare. Madanlal was a misguided young man, about 20 years of age, but he appeared to have little or no regard for the sanctity of human life, and thus the bench did not see any reason for commending his case to the Crown for the exercise of the power of clemency.

Referring to the defence plea that there was no conspiracy to murder Mahatma Gandhi, Justice Bhandari observed, 'The mass of evidence that has been produced in this case leaves no doubt in my mind that all the prisoners, with the exception of Parchure and Shankar, had entered into an agreement to take the life of Mahatma Gandhi.'

The Judge said, 'The evidence which has been produced in this case makes it quite clear that Nathuram, Apte, Karkare, Madanlal and Badge had a motive to obtain revolvers from Dadaji Maharaj; that Nathuram and Apte made similar efforts to obtain revolvers from Badge, Dixitji Maharaj and Gopal; that on 13 January 1948 Nathurarn assigned his policies in the names of the wife of Apte and the wife of Gopal; that on or about 10 January 1948 Madanlal took Karkare to the house of Dr Jain and introduced Karkare as a "seth" from Ahmednagar; and that on or about 12 January 1948 Madanlal told Dr Jain that he and others of his party had decided to assassinate Mahatma Gandhi.'

Badge testified to a number of statements which made it quite clear that the prisoners wanted to take the life of Mahatma Gandhi. On 14 January 1948, Apte met Badge on the road near the Hindu Mahasabha office and said that it was good that he had come and that arrangement would have to be made for keeping the 'stuff'. On 15 January 1948, Apte asked Badge if he was prepared to go with them to Delhi saying that Savarkar had decided that Mahatma Gandhi, Pandit Nehru and Suhrawardy should be 'finished' and that he had entrusted the work to Nathuram and Apte.

Several criticisms had been directed towards the evidence of Dr J C Jain. It was contended in the first place that as Dr Jain was aware on or about 12 January 1948 that a serious offence was likely to be committed and as he omitted to transmit this information to the authorities without loss of time he should be regarded as an accomplice, whose statement could not be accepted without corroboration.

Justice Bhandari observed, 'I regret I am unable to concur in this view. An accomplice is *prima facie* a person who is concerned in the commission of a crime and the burden of proving a person to be an accomplice is on the person who alleges him to be one, namely, the prisoner. That burden has not been discharged in the present case. Dr Jain did not agree to the commission of the crime and he did not facilitate the commission of one. On the other hand, it seems to me that he strained every nerve to prevent it. As soon as he heard that Madanlal and the members of his party were entertaining designs on the life of Mahatma Gandhi he told Madanlal not to behave like a child. He told him that being a refugee from the Punjab, and having gone through a terrible amount of suffering he was incapable of viewing things in the true perspective. He had a long talk with Madanlal and tried to dissuade him from what he said he was going to do. He warned him of the folly of pursuing a plan which was fraught with such dangerous consequences. He endeavoured to prevail upon him to halt at the threshold of crime. Madanlal thanked Dr Jain for his advice and gave him to understand that if he did not listen to his advice he would be doomed. When Dr Jain saw in the papers that a bomb had exploded in Birla House and that Madanlal has been arrested in connection with the explosion, the seriousness of the situation dawned upon him. He lost no time in communicating with the authorities and placing his services unreservedly at their disposal for bringing the offenders to book. That was not the conduct of a person who had concurred in the commission of the crime. I am clearly of the opinion that Dr Jain is not an accomplice and his statement does not need to be corroborated.'

The second criticism was that the evidence of Dr Jain could not be accepted at its face value, because he made a considerable delay in reporting the matter to the police or other appropriate authorities. The so-called extra-judicial confession was made to him on or about 12 January 1948 but he did not inform either the police or any higher authority till 21 January 1948, i.e., a day after the bomb had exploded at Delhi.

A certain amount of delay was occasioned, but the facts and circumstances of the case made it quite clear that he had reasonable grounds for not rushing to make a report against Madanlal. In the first place, Dr Jain did not attach any importance to the statement made by Madanlal, (a) because Madanlal was given to a certain amount of bragging and (b) because a great deal of loose talk was going on in those days. Secondly, Angad Singh told Dr Jain not to attach any importance to Madanlal's statement. Thirdly, Madanlal himself told him on the following day that he had thought over the advice given to him that he was under an obligation to Dr Jain that he regarded him as his father and that he had no intention of pursuing the plan. Fourthly, Madanlal saw Dr Jain immediately before leaving for Delhi and did not mention anything about the designs on the life of Mahatma Gandhi. Fifthly, Dr Jain had reason to believe that Madanlal was an honest and straightforward person and that Madanlal would honour the words of his adviser as he held Dr Jain in high esteem.

A person who was so honest and straightforward in his dealings with Dr Jain, and who was so deeply indebted to him, could not be expected to let down his friend and benefactor. Dr Jain was naturally reluctant to report Madanlal to the police. Indeed, Dr Jain appeared to have believed that there was nothing in the plan which had been unfolded to him.

The third criticism was that the story narrated was intrinsically improbable. The prosecution alleges that Madanlal went to Poona on 9 January 1948 to examine arms and ammunition, and it was accordingly argued that if it was true that he went there on 9 January 1948 and if it was true that he disclosed the entire plan to Dr Jain on 12 or 13 January 1948, he could not have omitted to inform Dr Jain of his visit to Poona. Madanlal made no such statement to Dr Jain and it was accordingly contended that the story narrated by Dr Jain could not be accepted as gospel truth. Dr Jain was not cross-examined in regard to Madanlal's visit to Poona, but if he had been cross-examined and if he said that Madanlal did not refer to his visit to Poona, the judge viewed that he would have attached any importance to the omission. Madanlal had just started the story about the conspiracy when Dr Jain interrupted him and asked him not to behave like a child. Again, it was argued that Madanlal could not have stated to Dr Jain on 12 or 13 January 1948 that he had been entrusted with the task of igniting the gun-cotton slab when the part that each particular conspirator was to play was not assigned till the afternoon of 20 January 1948.

This argument did carry force, but was it beyond the realms of probability that certain tentative decisions (which were to be finalised after the inspection of the spot) were taken early in January 1948. The prosecution alleged that as early as 10 January 1948 Nathuram and Apte had already placed an order with Badge for the supply of two gun-cotton slabs and five hand-grenades. This order could be placed if and only if Nathuram and

Apte had evolved some sort of plan. It was by no means improbable that the conspirators had vaguely planned that a gun-cotton slab could be exploded and that the explosion should be caused by Madanlal. Even if no specific part was assigned to Madanlal till 20 January 1948, he might have thought, in view of his exploit at Ahmednagar and particularly in view of the manner in which he had handled the Muslims of that town that the important task of throwing the bomb would be entrusted to him.

The fourth objection that has been taken on behalf of the defence appears to carry much greater force. It was said that Dr Jain had testified to at least two incidents before the Trial Court which were not mentioned either to Angad Singh on 13 or 14 January 1948, or to Morarji Desai on 21 January 1948, or to the Presidency Magistrate on 26 January 1948. He stated before the Trial Court that when Madanlal saw him on or about 12 January 1948, he said that he had been entrusted with the work of throwing a bomb at the prayer meeting of Gandhiji to create a confusion and that in the confusion so caused Gandhiji was to be overpowered by the members of his party. This was the statement attributed by Dr Jain to Madanlal in the Court of the Special Judge. The statement attributed to Madanlal before Angad Singh, Morarji Desai and the Presidency Magistrate was the bare statement that the party to which Madanlal belonged had plotted to do away with the great leader and that the leader was Mahatma Gandhi. No mention was made of the fact that a bomb was to be thrown to create confusion or that in the confusion so created Mahatma Gandhi was to be overpowered or that the task of throwing the bomb had been entrusted to Madanlal. Indeed no mention was made of the precise method in which the object which the conspirators had in view was to be achieved.

The second statement which was attributed to Madanlal was that he told Dr Jain that his companions were staying at the Hindu Mahasabha office at Dadar. No such statement was made by Dr Jain either to Angad Singh or to Morarji Desai or to the Presidency Magistrate. Unfortunately, neither Angad Singh nor Morarji Desai kept a record of the statements of Dr Jain and might have forgotten the details when they gave evidence in the Court after the lapse of seven months; but even so it seemed highly improbable that if the statements which were attributed to Madanlal had been made by him, these two witnesses could have forgotten them. The omission of the statements from the depositions of Dr Jain under Section 164 Cr P C could be readily understood. Daphtary, the Chief Prosecution Counsel, explained that such statements were not recorded by magistrates in the city of Bombay and that the magistrate who was called upon to record the statement of Dr Jain was not conversant with the procedure which was prevalent in Punjab. He accordingly contented himself by preparing a memorandum of the statement made by Dr Jain and scrupulously avoided the insertion of details. This explanation was fully supported by the statement Exhibit DII which Dr Jain was said to have made. The statement was brief, sketchy and disjointed and contained nothing, but the most important facts. It did not give even the more important details, such as that Madanlal had been collecting arms and ammunition which had been dumped in a jungle or that he had committed an assault on Rao Saheb Patwardhan or that

Veer Savarkar had sent for him or that Dr Jain had narrated the story to Angad Singh.

Dr Jain was in a very peculiar position owing partly to the courage and integrity of his own character. He had given every possible help and encouragement to Madanlal who had lost everything in Pakistan and Madanlal, on the other hand, entertained a very warm regard, which almost verged on adoration for Dr Jain. Impetuous, sentimental and boastful as he was, Madanlal happened to blurt out in a moment of weakness the secret which his companions were so anxious to preserve. This was done obviously in a spirit of bravado and possibly in the hope that his statement would be received with approbation by his patron and friend. The response was completely contrary to his expectations. Approbation was replaced by reprobation and appreciation by condemnation. Madanlal hastened to retrace his step, but the mischief had been done. The arrow had been shot and could not be recalled. What did Madanlal do in the circumstances? He assured Dr Jain that in view of the regard that he entertained for him he had decided to listen to his advice and to abandon the plan. Dr Jain did not know whether to believe him or not. He was on the horns of a dilemma and the prey of conflicting emotions.

In this state of mind Dr Jain allowed things to drift, not knowing what to do. When the bomb exploded in Delhi on 20 January 1948, he realised the seriousness of the mistake committed by him. He realised that the information given by Madanlal was something more than the irresponsible prattle of a refugee. He rose to the occasion. He shouldered the burden of the inevitable consequences and did his duty to the society. After the death of Mahatma Gandhi, he came openly into the field and told Morarji Desai that he was prepared to help the police regardless of the consequences to himself. He had no desire to conceal his name. He had no axe of his own to grind. He was not under the influence of the police. He had no reason to think that merely because he had been helping Madanlal he was in danger of being implicated in the crime. He had been a very staunch Congressman, for he was detained in custody during the Quit India Movement of 1942. The judge observed, 'I have read his statement over and over again and every time I read it, the conviction grows in my mind that he is telling nothing but the truth. His statement is simple and clear, the incidents he relates are probable and consistent, the story he gives fits in the story narrated by Badge, like a jigsaw puzzle.'

The learned Judge continued, 'The mass of evidence that has been produced in this case leaves no doubt that all the prisoners (with the exception of Parchure and Shankar) had entered into an agreement to take the life of Mahatma Gandhi.'

The evidence against Nathuram and Apte was that they placed an order with Badge for the supply of arms and ammunition; that they examined the articles which were brought by Badge in the presence of Dixitji Maharaj; that they paid various sums of money to Badge for carrying out the purpose of conspiracy; that they travelled to Delhi and stayed in the Marina Hotel under assumed names; that they held a conference in Marina Hotel at which various details in regard to the execution of the plan were settled; that they actually went to Birla House in the afternoon of 20 January 1948 with the object of supervising the operations; and that when they found that the plan had failed they immediately left the hotel and reached Bombay via Cawnpore (Kanpur). In Bombay, they stayed under assumed names. On 27 January 1948, they again left Bombay by air, under assumed names, and came to Delhi from where they proceeded to Gwalior; that they obtained a pistol from Gwalior and came back to Delhi to put themselves in possession of the opportunity of assassinating Mahatma Gandhi.

Nathuram admitted having gone to the Birla House in the afternoon of 30 January 1948 and fired three shots at Mahatma Gandhi. He denied, however, the existence of a conspiracy. On the other hand, he accepted the entire blame for the unfortunate incident of 30 January 1948 and stated that he alone and no one else should be punished. He further stated that their object throughout was to stage a peaceful demonstration but that after the failure of the plan of 20 January 1948, he secretly decided that the only method of stopping Mahatma Gandhi from his pro-Muslim policy was to assassinate him. Once his mind was made up, he came to the railway station at Delhi, booked a room for himself in order to ponder over the future plans. Nathuram stated that he did not take Apte into his confidence and that Apte was not aware of what he was about to do.

In view of the judges, 'It is not necessary to go into an elaborate examination of the witnesses who have appeared in evidence against Nathuram and Apte, for I am satisfied that there was a conspiracy to kill Mahatma Gandhi. If that conspiracy was in existence, there can be little doubt that both Nathuram and Apte were members thereof.'

Broadly speaking the evidence against Karkare was that on 9 January 1948, Karkare and certain other persons

examined some 'stuff' at the shop of Badge; that on or
about 10 January 1948 Madanlal took Karkare to the
house of Dr Jagdishchandra Jain and introduced Karkare
as a 'seth' from Ahmednagar; that on 15 January 1948
Karkare accompanied Nathuram, Apte, Madanlal and
Badge to the house of Dixitji Maharaj and examined some
arms and ammunition which had been brought by Badge
and handed over the bag containing the said arms and
ammunition to Madanlal for being taken to Delhi; that
on the same day Karkare and Madanlal left Bombay for
Delhi by the night train; that Karkare told Amchekar that
he was a worker of the Hindu Mahasabha and was going
to Delhi for some work of the Mahasabha; that on arrival
at Delhi at 12.30 pm on 17 January 1948, Karkare,
Madanlal and Amchekar stayed at Sharif Hotel in
Chandni Chowk, Delhi where Karkare stayed under an
assumed name—'B. M. Bias'; that on 18 January 1948,
Karkare told Amchekar that he was going to the railway
station as he expected somebody; that Gopal Godse
visited Karkare and Madanlal at Sharif Hotel on 18
January 1948; that Karkare told Amchekar on 19 January
1948 that he and Madanlal were leaving the hotel the
same day and spending the night in Maharashtra Niwas
and were leaving for Jullundur on the following morning
in connection with the marriage of Madanlal; that
Karkare went to Marina Hotel on various occasions
between 17 and 20 January 1948, visited Nathuram and
Apte on more than one occasion and was served with
tea and alcoholic drinks at Marina Hotel; that on 20
January 1948, Karkare and Apte visited Hindu
Mahasabha Bhawan, on more than one occasion, handed
over the bag containing arms and ammunition which had
been brought from Bombay to Delhi for being taken to

Marina Hotel; that Karkare was present at the conference in Marina Hotel and was given a hand-grenade for being thrown on Mahatma Gandhi; that at about 5 o'clock on the afternoon of 20 January 1948 Karkare and Madanlal reached Birla House; that Karkare endeavoured to obtain admission into the room containing the trellis-window; that on 25 January 1948 he went to the house of G M Joshi at Thana, near Bombay and conferred with Nathuram, Apte and Gopal; and that on 29 and 30 January 1948 he was seen in a retiring room at the Delhi railway station along with Nathuram and Apte.

Dange, who appeared for Karkare, contended that his client was involved in this case because like Savarkar he was actively associated with the work of Hindu Mahasabha. Dange viewed that his client had denied that he had committed any offence, and the prosecution had failed to prove the case against him beyond reasonable doubt and that Karkare had given satisfactory explanation of the circumstances appearing in evidence against him. According to Dange, only a few witnesses had appeared against Karkare in so far as the incidents in Delhi were concerned. These witnesses were Nain Singh and Gobind Ram, who saw Karkare in Marina Hotel on 17 and 18 January 1948, Chottu Ram and Bhur Singh, who saw him in Birla House on 20 January 1948 and Sundarilal, Hari Kishan and Janu who were alleged to have seen Karkare at the railway station at Delhi on 29 and 30 January 1948. The case which he had set out to establish on behalf of his client was that Karkare went to Delhi in connection with the proposed marriage of Madanlal; that while at Delhi, Madanlal induced him to give his moral support to a demonstration which the refugees of Delhi were about to stage; that Karkare expressed his willingness to go to Birla House as he was opposed to the pro-Muslim policy of Mahatma Gandhi, but that he declined to take any active part, as a detention order had already been issued against him; and that he was unable to reach Birla House, on 20 January 1948, as he was a stranger to the town and lost his way in the confusing and bewildering network of streets for which Delhi was known. The trial court had come to the conclusion that although Karkare was present in Delhi on 29 and 30 January 1948, he did not go to Birla House on the date on which Mahatma Gandhi was assassinated.

The judge viewed that, 'after carefully going through the evidence in the case, I have come to the conclusion that Nathuram, Apte, Karkare, Madanlal and Badge had entered into an agreement to take the life of Mahatma Gandhi and that in pursuance of this agreement, they collected arms and ammunition and proceeded to Delhi. The evidence which has already been commented upon shows that Karkare, Madanlal and certain other persons examined the "stuff" in the shop of Badge at Poona on 9 January 1948; that Karkare accompanied Nathuram, Apte and others to the house of Dixitji Maharaj where Badge had brought the "stuff" for being taken to Delhi; that Karkare took the bag containing the "stuff" and made it over to Madanlal. Karkare admits that he accompanied him to Delhi and put up in Sharif Hotel, where the room occupied by them was shared by Amchekar. The question which requires consideration is whether he went there with the object of facilitating the marriage of Madanlal, as alleged by him.'

The judge continued, 'I consider Amchekar to be a highly independent and respectable witness. This witness states that on their arrival at Delhi on Saturday, 17

January 1948, they proceeded to Sharif Hotel where
Karkare, Madanlal and the witness booked a room for
themselves, Karkare giving his name as "B M Bias". Some
two hours later Karkare left the hotel saying that he was
going to Hindu Mahasabha Bhawan. Madanlal and the
witness, who were left behind, went to Chandni Chowk
where Madanlal wanted to see an uncle. It is not known
whether Karkare returned to the hotel for the night, but
he was certainly back in the hotel on Sunday morning,
for he told Amchekar that he was proceeding to the
railway station as he was expecting someone. Madanlal
and the witness went to various places, both on the
morning and the evening of Sunday, including the house
of the prospective bride of Madanlal. They also went to
attend a meeting which was to be addressed by Pandit
Jawaharlal Nehru and Jayaprakash Narayan. Karkare
does not appear to have slept in the hotel on the night
of Sunday, 18 January 1948, for he was absent the whole
day; he was absent when the witness retired for the
night and he was absent when the witness left his bed
on the following morning. He did not come back till after
the witness had gone away in connection with his
business. He appears to have returned to the hotel
sometime later for when the witness returned from the
Transfer Bureau at 3.00 pm on 19 January 1948, he found
Karkare and Madanlal talking to a stranger (Gopal)
inside the room. Karkare told the witness that both
Madanlal and he were leaving the hotel at once as they
had decided to spend the night in Maharashtra Niwas
and to leave for Jullundur, a district town in Punjab, on
the following morning in connection with the marriage
of Madanlal. The witness paid his share of the hotel bill
to Karkare and left the hotel at 5.00 pm. It is said that

Karkare and Madanlal left the hotel two hours later after taking back the clothes which they had given for washing.'

The appellate bench observed that the evidence of this witness made it quite clear that Karkare came to Delhi not with the object of facilitating the marriage of Madanlal, but some other object which was stated by the prosecution to be the desire to promote the objects of the conspiracy. If Karkare had come to Delhi in connection with the marriage of Madanlal he would have done something in connection with that. He did not appear to have taken the slightest interest in the matter. As stated above, he left the hotel at about 4 o'clock on the afternoon of Saturday, 17 January 1948, and was away the whole afternoon and possibly also the evening. He did not accompany Madanlal to the house of his uncle. On the following morning, Karkare intimated his intention of going to the railway station as he was expecting someone. He did not put in an appearance during the whole of Sunday, 18 January 1948. Madanlal and Amchekar, however, went out to various places including the house of the prospective bride. Karkare did not return to the hotel at night and was not back in the hotel till the following morning. On the contrary, the evidence of Marina Hotel witnesses proved beyond reasonable doubt that Karkare had been served a drink at Marina Hotel on 17 January 1948 and two drinks at the said hotel on 18 January 1948. This evidence showed that Karkare was in fact visiting Marina Hotel. The prosecution alleged that he actually spent the night of 18 January 1948 in the said hotel.

Examining the story that Karkare and Madanlal were spending the night of 19 January 1948 in Maharashtra

Niwas and were proceeding to Jullundur on the following morning in connection with the marriage of Madanlal, there was not an iota of evidence on the record to show that after Karkare and Madanlal left Sharif Hotel at about 7.00 pm on 19 January 1948, they went to Maharashtra Niwas. On the other hand, the evidence of Badge shows that Madanlal and Gopal were in Hindu Mahasabha Bhawan, when Badge and Shankar arrived from Bombay. Badge stated further that Nathuram, Apte and Karkare came to Bhawan at night and told him that they had been to the railway station, but had not been able to see Badge and Shankar. Nathuram, Apte and Karkare left shortly afterwards promising to call at the Bhawan on the following morning. Madanlal and Gopal spent the night of 19 January 1948 in Mahasabha Bhawan along with Badge and Shankar. It had not been contended that Karkare and Madanlal left for Jullundur on the following morning. On the other hand, it had been proved conclusively that Madanlal was in Delhi on 20 January 1948, for he ignited a gun-cotton slab at Birla House at around 5 o'clock in the afternoon of that date and was immediately arrested. A live hand-grenade was recovered from his possession. The only conclusion that could be drawn from the statement of Amchekar, which was fully corroborated by the other circumstances of the case, was that Karkare was anxious to conceal from Amchekar the real object of their visit to Delhi. Neither he nor Madanlal had any intention of spending the night of 19 January 1948 at Maharashtra Niwas or of proceeding to Jullundur the following morning.

Karkare's presence in Birla House on the afternoon of 20 January 1948 was established by the evidence of Chottu Ram. On the day of the occurrence, Bhur Singh, the watchman at the Birla House, was sitting on a takhtposh (wooden four-leg bedstead) in front of the room through the trellis-window of which the conspirators had proposed to throw the hand-grenades. He stated that a car drove into the open circular space behind Birla House and four passengers alighted. They started talking to some persons who were standing near the gate of Birla House. One of them (whom he later identified as Karkare) went up to the witness and asked him for permission to take a photograph through the trellis-work of the window. The witness told him that no useful purpose was likely to be served by taking a photograph from the back of Mahatma Gandhi. He offered a small bribe to the witness, which the latter denied. An explosion took place a few minutes later.

Although Badge did not state that Karkare was carrying a bag on 20 January 1948, but a bag could have come into his hands in any one of several ways. For example, the bag which Badge was carrying could have been handed over to Karkare temporarily. Again Karkare might have brought a bag with him from Bombay in his steel trunk or he might have purchased one in Delhi. A grenade was given to Karkare at Marina Hotel. Chottu Ram was positive that the man who addressed him was Karkare and that Karkare was carrying a bag. It was further stated that on 28 and 29 January 1948, Karkare was seen at the railway station of Delhi in the company of Nathuram and Apte.

When the witness was invited to the parade, which was held on 2 February 1948, he picked up Karkare and Apte and said that on the day of the explosion in Birla House four persons including Karkare and Apte had come to Birla House at 4.30 or 5.00 pm, and that he stated before the trial court on a later date that Karkare was the person who had made the request of taking the photograph.

The next piece of evidence against Karkare was that on the morning of Sunday, 25 January 1948, he appeared at the house of his friend and relation C M Joshi at Thana, Bombay and asked him to have a telegram dispatched to Apte requesting Nathuram and Apte to see him in Thana. Gopal also came and took part in the conference which was held at about 9 o'clock in the night. The nature of the conversations which took place had not been indicated but there can be little doubt that the prisoners surveyed the situation as a result of the arrest of Madanlal and completed their plans for the future.

The judge was convinced that the evidence on record satisfied him that Karkare was a member of the conspiracy to take the life of Mahatma Gandhi and that he had been rightly convicted.

The case against Madanlal is that he was opposed to the pro-Muslim policy of Mahatma Gandhi; that while at Ahmednagar, he came into contact with Karkare who entertained similar views; that both Karkare and Madanlal went to the shop of Badge in Poona with the object of inspecting the arms and ammunition which were being offered for sale; that on or about 12 January 1948, he made all extra judicial confession to Dr J C Jain telling him that he had been entrusted with the work of throwing a bomb at the prayer meeting of Mahatmaji to create a confusion and that in the confusion so created Mahatmaji was to be overpowered by the members of his party; that on 15 January 1948, he accompanied Nathuram, Apte, Karkare and Badge to the house of Dixitji Maharaj where Badge showed the explosives which he had brought from Poona; that the bag containing the explosives was then entrusted to his care with the object of being taken to Delhi; that the same night he accompanied Karkare to Delhi; that on 19 January 1948, he joined Karkare in making a false representation to Amchekar that both Karkare and Madanlal were shifting to Maharashtra Niwas the same evening and were leaving for Jullundur on the following morning; that on the evening of 19 January 1948, he stayed in Hindu Mahasabha Bhawan along with Gopal, Badge and Shankar; that on 20 January 1948 he accompanied Karkare to Marina Hotel and joined the conference that was held there; that a gun-cotton slab and a hand-grenade were handed over to him with the direction that on a signal being given by Nathuram and Apte, he was to explode the gun-cotton slab and to throw the hand-grenade; that he ignited the gun-cotton slab and was immediately arrested; and that a live hand-grenade was recovered from his possession.

Madanlal denied the correctness of circumstances appearing in evidence against him. He admitted having gone to Delhi with Karkare, but he stated that he went there in connection with his marriage. Madanlal also admitted that he went to Birla House on 20 January 1948, but he did so with the object of making a peaceful demonstration. On being asked to explain the circumstances in which he came into possession of a live hand-grenade, Madanlal stated that Badge had given him a gun-cotton-slab and hand-grenade as samples for sale to refugees.

Based on the evidence furnished by the prosecution in support of the testimony of the approver, the Appeal Court viewed that there was no doubt that Madanlal was a member of the conspiracy which was formed to take the life of Mahatma Gandhi. Madanlal took an active part in procuring arms and ammunition and transporting them from Bombay to Delhi. He made a confession to Dr J C Jain which showed almost conclusively that a conspiracy was in existence and that the conspirators had planned to assassinate Mahatma Gandhi. It was true that he did not take a prominent part in connection with the conspiracy on 17, 18 and 19 January 1948, but he took a leading part in the execution of the plans on the following day. Madanlal went to the Marina Hotel, where he put on a coat belonging to Apte and later proceeded with Karkare to the prayer ground where he ignited the gun-cotton slab. He was caught red-handed with a live hand-grenade in his pocket. If his object was merely to make a peaceful demonstration, he would have run up to Mahatma Gandhi immediately after he had lighted the fuse. Even if he did not rush towards Mahatmaji then, he could have run to him as soon as the slab had exploded and could have ventilated the grievances which he was so keen to bring to the notice of the Mahatma. He did nothing of the kind. His conduct at the prayer-ground was wholly inconsistent with the theory that he went to the prayer-ground with the object of only making a demonstration. Again, the explanation given by him in regard to the recovery of a live hand-grenade was hollow and unconvincing.

Bannerji, who appeared for Madanlal, contended that assuming for the sake of argument that Madanlal was a member of the conspiracy, he ceased to be one as soon as he was arrested by the police on 20 January 1948.

The Appeal Court did not accept this contention since the crime of conspiracy would consist in an agreement between two or more persons to do a criminal act. If, therefore, anything was being done in pursuance of that agreement, all the members who were parties to the agreement would be equally liable for the acts of others. In such cases every conspirator would be presumed in the eye of law to be an agent of the others. But it was open to a conspirator to withdraw from the conspiracy and thus relieve himself from a homicide committed subsequent to the said withdrawal provided he notified his associates of such withdrawal. It was true that Madanlal was arrested on 20 January 1948 and that it was not possible for him to give an effective help to the conspirators in achieving the object of the conspiracy, but it was not necessary for every member of a conspiracy to take an active interest in the execution of the common purpose. Silent parties were by no means an uncommon feature of conspiracies. If Madanlal had dissociated himself from the conspirators and had made his intention known to his associates either by express words or by his conduct, it might have been possible to argue that he was not responsible for the murder which was committed after the date of his disavowal or dissociation. But Madanlal never informed his co-conspirators that he had abandoned the common purpose. The court further viewed that it was impossible for him to escape the liability for the criminal acts committed by his confederates and the circumstances of the case left no doubt that the charges were brought home to Madanlal beyond reasonable doubt.

Briefly summarised the evidence against Gopal Godse, it was established that on 14 January 1948 his brother Nathuram effected a nomination of his life policy for a sum of Rs 3,000 in favour of Mrs Sindhutai, wife of Gopal; that on the same date Gopal applied for seven days' casual leave from 15 to 21 January 1948 for some immediate farm affairs at his village; that seven days' casual leave was granted to him with effect from 17 January 1948; that on the afternoon of 19 January 1948 he paid a visit to Karkare and Madanlal who were putting up in Sharif Hotel, Delhi; that on the night of 19 January 1948 he stayed with Madanlal in a room of Hindu Mahasabha Bhawan, Delhi; that on the morning of 20 January 1948, Apte took Gopal, Badge and Shankar to the jungle behind Mahasabha Bhawan for trying out the two revolvers which had been brought by Gopal and Badge; that after his return to Mahasabha Bhawan he accompanied Apte, Badge and Shankar to Marina Hotel with the Khaki bag in which Madanlal had brought the 'stuff' from Bombay to Delhi together with the revolver which Gopal had brought with him from Karkare; that on arriving in Room no 40 of Marina Hotel, Gopal started repairing his revolver while Apte, Karkare, Madanlal and Badge started fixing primers to the gun-cotton slabs and detonators to the hand-grenades; that in his presence and within his hearing Nathuran told Badge that this was their last effort; that the work should be accomplished and that they should see that everything was done properly. While they were still in the room the various parts which the conspirators were to take at Birla House were assigned to them and arms and ammunition were distributed; that a hand-grenade was given to Gopal with the object that it should be thrown at Mahatma Gandhi as soon as commotion was caused by the explosion of the slab; that Gopal accompanied Apte, Badge and Shankar in a taxi belonging to Surjit Singh from Regal Cinema to Hindu Mahasabha Bhawan; that

Gopal went inside the Bhawan and left his bag containing the ammunition in the cupboard of his room; that the party proceeded by the same taxi to the back gate of Birla House and met Nathuram, Karkare and Madanlal; that in the presence of Gopal, Apte asked Madanlal whether he was ready; that Madanlal replied that he was ready since he had placed the gun-cotton slab and that it remained only to be ignited; that Karkare came and told Apte that he had made arrangements with Chottu Ram to allow someone to enter that room as a photographer; that Badge refused to enter that room for fear of being trapped inside, and intimated his desire to shoot from the open; that after the explosion, Nathuram, Apte and Gopal entered the taxi and left immediately for Connaught Place; that Gopal stayed at Frontier Hotel, Delhi, under the assumed name 'Rajagopalan' on the night of 20 and 21 January 1948; that Karkare also stayed in the same hotel that night under the assumed name— 'P V Godbole' of Poona and deposited a revolver and bullets with him; that on or about 24 January 1948, Gopal met Nathuram and Apte in Hotel Elphinstone Annexe, Bombay; that at about 4 o'clock on the afternoon of 25 January 1948, he went to the house of G M Joshi at Thana, Bombay with a trunk, and met Nathuram, Apte and Karkare; that he rejoined his post on the morning of 27 January 1948; that Mahatma Gandhi was assassinated on 30 January 1948 by his brother Nathuram; that when he was arrested in his native village of Uksan on 5 February 1948, he was found to be in possession of the bag in which Badge had taken the 'stuff' from Poona to Bombay and which had been brought by Madanlal from Bombay to Delhi; that Gopal was identified by Govind Melekar on 2 March 1948, Amchekar on 16 March 1948,

Mehar Singh and Ram Parkash on 24 March 1948, Ram Lal Dutt, Surjit Singh, Shanti Prakash and Gobind Ram on 30 March and Bhur Singh on 31 March 1948.

Gopal admitted that his brother Nathuram effected a nomination of insurance policy in favour of his wife but stated that he was not aware of this nomination; he admitted having applied for leave but he stated that his leave was spent in his native village; he denied having visited Delhi or having been there between 17 and 21 January 1948; he further denied having visited the house of Godbole of Poona or Elphinstone Hotel Annexe or having gone to Thana, Bombay; he denied that a bag was recovered from his possession when he was arrested near Uksan. He admitted that he was identified by various witnesses on the dates mentioned above, but complained that he was shown to the witnesses prior to each identification. On being questioned as to why the witnesses had given evidence against him he stated that the witnesses had deposed against him under the pressure of the police. No evidence was produced in defence.

The first important piece of evidence against Gopal was that on 14 January 1948 his brother Nathuram effected a nomination of his policy in favour of Mrs Sindhutai, wife of Gopal. It was no crime on the part of a brother-in-law to assign a policy in favour of his sister-in-law, but it was a curious-coincidence that this policy should be assigned on 14 January 1948; that a sum of Rs 250 should be paid to Gopal by his brother on the same date and that he should apply for leave on the same date. The prosecution alleged that Nathuram assigned his policy in favour of the wife of Gopal in order that some provision should be made for her in the event of

Nathuram and Gopal being put out of the way by the decision of a judicial tribunal and that he paid a sum of Rs 250 to Gopal for the purchase of a revolver related to the conspiracy. It was said that Gopal applied for seven days' casual leave with effect from 14 January 1948 in order that he should be able to accompany Karkare and Madanlal from Bombay to Delhi on 15 January 1948. Gopal stated in his application that he wanted to take leave for some immediate farm affairs at his village, but this explanation did not appear to be plausible. If he did proceed on leave with effect from 17 January 1948 and did actually spend that leave in his native village, he could have had no difficulty in producing witnesses from his village to the effect that he was there during the whole of his leave. No evidence whatsoever was produced and no effort had been made to establish the plea of alibi.

On the other hand, convincing evidence had been produced on behalf of the prosecution to the effect that Gopal was in fact in Delhi on the afternoon of 19 January 1948 and during the whole of 20 January 1948.

Ram Lal Dutt, Shanti Parkash and Amchekar were the first set of witnesses who saw Gopal in Delhi. The first two were partners of Sharif Hotel, while the third was a refugee from Sind. Ram Lal Dutt stated that on 19 January 1948 a person came to enquire about the room in which Madanlal was staying. The witness had him sent to Room no 2 through a servant. Shanti Parkash deposed that on the same day he prepared a bill for 'B M Bias' and Karkare in respect of the charges payable to the hotel. Bias came to the office along with an outsider and asked the witness to furnish details of the account. He was given the necessary details and he paid the bill in full. Bias then came again to the office at about 2 pm and informed that he would leave the hotel sometime later. The witness told him that he would be charged the rent of the room for another day, but later reduced the rent at his request. Amchekar stated that when he returned from the Transfer Bureau at about 3 o'clock on the afternoon of 19 January 1948 and went to his room, he found Karkare and Madanlal with a stranger, whom he later identified as Gopal, sitting in the room. As soon as he entered the room, he was told by Karkare that Madanlal and he were going to vacate the room and that they were going to Maharashtra Niwas for the night and proceeding to Jullundur on the following morning. The witness told Karkare that he had finished his work and was going back to Bombay that very day and enquired from Karkare as to what his permanent address at Bombay was. Karkare replied that it was not necessary to furnish him with the address. Madanlal, however, had no hesitation in giving his own address, and he told the witness that he was residing at the Chembur Refugee Camp in Bombay. According to Amchekar, Gopal kept sitting in the room in the hotel with Karkare and Madanlal for about two hours during the whole period, with the exception of fifteen minutes. Amchekar himself was also in the same room. It was argued on behalf of the defence that Amchekar being a refugee from Sind, was a man of straw and consequently his evidence should not be accepted as gospel truth. Daphtary, however, contended that Amchekar was not an unreliable witness. A perusal of Exhibit P 12 made it quite clear that this witness, who was about thirty years of age, passed the Matriculation Examination of the Bombay University in 1936 and was working as Rationing Enquiry Inspector before the partition. He could read, speak and write Marathi and English and could read and speak Hindi and Gujarati. He had no reason to be hostile either to Madanlal or Gopal. If he had chosen to be hostile to either of these prisoners, he could have given much stronger evidence against them. The statement actually made by him did not betray any anxiety on his part to implicate Gopal. In the identification parade which was held on 20 March 1948, the witness picked up Gopal as the person whom he had seen in his room on 19 January 1948. He was, however, unable to give the name of Gopal as that name was not given to him at Delhi.

The Appeal Court viewed that Amchekar was intrinsically and inherently reliable and that there was no reason why his evidence should not be accepted as against Gopal. The Presiding Judge was not quite certain, however, whether the evidence of the two partners of Sharif Hotel was equally trustworthy. Daphtary contended that the allegation made against these witnesses that they were under the thumb of the police should be discounted. In their capacity as hotel managers it was their duty to come into contact with a large number of persons and to remember their faces. Again, it was stated that Madanlal had brought the police to Sharif Hotel on 23 January 1948 and as they were examined on that day the features of the person whom they had seen in the room of Madanlal must have been impressed on their memories. Indeed, it was stated that the allegation that Gopal came to the hotel that day was consistent with the probabilities of the case. Immediately on his arrival in Delhi, Gopal had seen Nathuram and Apte in Marina Hotel. Nathuram must have told Gopal to ask Karkare and Madanlal to leave the hotel and not to stay with Amchekar, who was a total stranger and who might later give evidence against them. It was said that Gopal must have gone to Sharif Hotel with the object of asking Karkare and Madanlal to leave the room and shift to another place. It was with that object that both Karkare and Madanlal informed Amchekar, as soon as he returned from the Transfer Bureau, that they were leaving the hotel the same afternoon spending the night in Maharashtra Niwas and proceeding to Jullundur on the following day.

Ramlal Dutt and Shanti Parkash were admittedly the partners of a hotel and possibly might be endowed with better memories than those of persons pursuing other callings, but it should be remembered that at least one of these persons, namely, Ram Lal Dutt started hotel business only with effect from 11 November 1947. His memory could not thus be said to have been so highly developed that he should remember a person whom he had seen only for a moment or so. The police enquired from him the description of the person who had come to see Madanlal and he told them that he would be able to identify the person if produced before him. He did not remember the description he had given of the person to the police. Shanti Prakash was more precise. He stated that the police enquired from him the description of the outsider and he gave the description of that outsider to the police. These persons were undoubtedly questioned on 23 January 1948 and the fact that they were questioned so shortly after 19 January 1948 might possibly have made them remember that a person had actually come to see Madanlal on 19 January 1948. It should be remembered, however, that they were not taken to Bombay till 30 March 1948 and it was extremely difficult for any person to identify another whom he had seen for a moment or so, seventy days before.

At the end, the Court opined that there was no reason to think that these witnesses were not telling the truth; however, the Court was of the opinion that it would not be safe to accept their testimony, without demur.

The next witness who saw Gopal in Delhi was Surjit Singh, who carried a certain number of passengers in his taxi from Regal Cinema to Birla Temple and from Birla Temple to Birla House and later from Birla House to Connaught Circus. This witness clearly identified Gopal as one of the passengers who travelled in his car on the date in question.

It would be seen from the above that the statement of Badge to the effect that Gopal came to Delhi was corroborated by at least five witnesses, namely, Ram Lal Dutt, Shanti Prakash, Amchekar, Surjit Singh and Bhur Singh. The evidence of these witnesses was strongly supported by the fact that Gopal took leave of absence at about the same time at which the other prisoners in this case were planning an attempt on the life of Mahatma Gandhi. Gopal was unable to provide any explanation whatsoever in regard to the place where he had spent his leave.

It was argued on behalf of Gopal Godse that he took no part whatsoever in the crime, for the bag containing his revolver and hand-grenade was left behind in the office of the Hindu Mahasabha and that he came to Delhi with the object of spending his leave with his brother. It was somewhat difficult to believe that Gopal would take a long and expensive journey from Poona to Delhi with no other object than that of seeing his brother. He did not state in his application that he wanted to visit Delhi.

It was unanimously held in the appeal that the prosecution had established beyond reasonable doubt that Gopal was a member of the conspiracy which was formed to assassinate Mahatma Gandhi. Nathuram effected a nomination of his life policy in favour of the wife of Gopal; that Gopal applied for leave on the same day; that Gopal had lunch with Nathuram at Poona on 14 January 1948 and applied at once for casual leave; and that Nathuram paid a sum of Rs 250 to Gopal; that Gopal was seen in Delhi was corroborated by the testimony of the witnesses, including Amchekar, Surjit Singh and Bhur Singh; that Gopal met Nathuram, Apte and Karkare at Thana, Bombay on 25 January 1948.

The date on which Gopal left Delhi was not known, but it appeared that he visited Nathuram and Apte at Elphinstone Hotel Annexe, Bombay, on or before 24 January 1948. G V Melekar, a bearer of the hotel, stated that Nathuram and Apte came to the hotel on 24 January 1948. The witness saw them on that day as well as on 25 January 1948 at about 7.00 am. They left the hotel on 27 January 1948 at about 6.30 am. On that date he had awakened them in the morning and had served them with tea and milk. While these two passengers were staying in the hotel, one gentleman, who was later identified as Gopal, came to visit them. The witness stated in cross-examination that this stranger had probably come on 25 January 1948. On the other hand, Vasant Joshi stated that Gopal was at his house visiting his father C M Joshi at about 4 o'clock in the afternoon of 25 January 1948. Much capital was made out of the fact that Gopal could not be in Bombay and in Thana, which are separated by a distance of 20 miles, at one and the same time. After carefully going through the depositions of these two witnesses namely, Melekar and Joshi, the Presiding Judge was satisfied that Gopal was in Thana on 25 January 1948 and could not have been in Bombay at the same hour on the same day. On the first occasion, he met Nathuram and Apte and on the second Nathuram, Apte and Karkare. He rejoined his duties on the morning of 26 January 1948 on the expiry of his leave. The news of Mahatma Gandhi's assassination was broadcast on 30 January 1948 and Gopal was in imminent danger of losing his own life as he was known to be a brother of the assassin. Police protection was given to him and he was sent away to his native village, Uksan. It appeared that on the arrest of Badge on 31 January 1948 and on Madanlal being brought to Bombay on or about the 4 February 1948, the police came to know that Gopal was also involved in the crime. He was arrested on 5 February 1948.

It was further argued on behalf of the prisoner that Gopal could not have taken part in the crime. In the first place, he was a Government servant who was perfectly settled in a Government post and who had no motives of the nature attributed to his brother Nathuram. Secondly, it was stated that Nathuram could have had no object in securing the help of Gopal. He did not want to make the wife of Gopal a widow by sending her husband to the gallows. Thirdly, it was said that no revolver, etc. had been traced to the possession of Gopal. Fourthly, it was alleged that Gopal was not assigned any part at the Marina Hotel conference, or if he was assigned any part he did not carry it out, for he left the revolver and the hand-grenade which were given to him at the Hindu Mahasabha office before leaving for Birla House. It might be that he did not take a prominent part in the execution of the common plan, but that fact would not exonerate him from blame and entitle him to escape from the liability of the persons who agreed to commit an unlawful act conjointly with others.

෧෩

Prisoners felicitated

On 12 November 1964, the city of Poona, which had a long tradition of spreading Hindutva was all set to welcome Gopal V Godse, Vishnu R Karkare and Madanlal K Pahwa released from prisons after the expiry of their sentences on 13 October 1964. Dr G V Ketkar, the grandson of Lokmanya Bal Gangadhar Tilak, the former editor of *Kesari* and the then editor of *Tarun Bharat*, a Poona based Marathi daily, was at the centre stage presiding over the *Satyavinayak Pooja* function at Udyan Hall facilitating the great heroes of the Gandhi murder conspiracy. Paying homage to Nathuram V Godse and Narayan D Apte, the patriots of the Hindu Nation, Ketkar disclosed that he knew about the plot from Nathuram at least six months prior to the ghastly deed. Gopal Godse, sitting next to him on the dais whispered to him, 'Don't speak anything more,' yet the old Mahasabhaite continued that he, in fact, apprised the late Balukaka Kanitkar, a prominent figure in Poona Congress circle, about the conspiracy hatched by some young fanatics of Hindu Mahasabha. Kanitkar, as Ketkar recollected, in turn had informed the late B G Kher, the then Premier of Bombay province, but the government did not take any steps to pre-empt the great happening.[19]

Indian Express in its edition on 14 November 1964 published the lead news condemning the Poona Reception, particularly the revelations made by Ketkar saying that Ketkar's fore-knowledge of the assassination only added to the mystery of the circumstances preceding the heinous crime. A nationwide furore followed for not only praising the murderers of the Father of the Nation, but also for their associates being regarded as national heroes as well. A detention order was issued by the then District Magistrate, Poona but Ketkar was at large. On 25 November 1964, however, Ketkar himself surrendered before the Commissioner of Police, Madras and he was brought to Yervada Jail in Poona.

Indignant questions were asked both in the Maharashtra Legislative Assembly and the Parliament demanding a thorough probe where Bhupesh Gupta's speech in the Parliament caused much embarrassment to the government. 'I should like to know whether after having failed to protect Mahatma Gandhi's life, we are today going to allow these kinds of things . . .! All these things have to be explained,' Gupta thundered in the Parliament.

Inquiry Commission set up

Appreciating the uproar across the geographic territory, Gulzarilal Nanda, the then Home Minister assured that since Balukaka Kanitkar was said to have passed (the information) to B G Kher (by this time who was also deceased), a detailed judicial enquiry would be undertaken and thus Gopal Sawrup Pathak, a Senior

Advocate of the Supreme Court was appointed to inquire into the conspiracy leading to the murder of Mahatma Gandhi.

On Pathak's appointment as a minister in the Union cabinet of India and subsequently the Governor of the state of Maharashtra, Justice J L Kapur, a retired judge of the Supreme Court of India on 21 November 1966 took over the charge of the inquiry.

Justice Kapur Commission took almost three years to complete the investigations on 30 September 1969 examining 101 witnesses after perusing 407 documents travelling to Delhi, Bombay, Nagpur, Dharwar, Poona, Baroda and Chandigarh. G V Ketkar was examined first followed by Desai and Nagarwala, the key witnesses who had deposed before the Commission for 15 and 7 days respectively. It was on 30 September 1969 that the investigation came to an end.

Negligence surfaced

In reality, Bombay administration had received as many as three grave warnings about the danger to the life of Mahatma. First, a registered letter from Balukaka Kanitkar containing crucial information had reached B G Kher in July 1947. Secondly, the information was passed over to both B G Kher and Morarji Desai in person by Prof J C Jain on 21 January 1948, and the third and the most important clue was received from Madanlal in custody on and from 20-24 January 1948 who had revealed the murder conspiracy in details and led the police contingents to several hideouts in Delhi.

M G Kanitkar, son of the late Balukaka Kanitkar, while deposing before the Kapur Commission confirmed that his father had sent a detailed letter, a warning indeed, to B G Kher and he himself had posted the registered letter. Morarji Desai also stated in the Commission that the information received from Balukaka Kanitkar was discussed at the meeting chaired by B G Kher where besides Desai, V T Dahejia, the then Home Secretary was also present. Nobody could ever know what had happened to the letter containing such vital information and that which was received at least six months prior to the assassination.[20] R B Kotwal, the appointed counsel for the Bombay Government, made his best effort to defend Desai arguing that the then Home Minister had passed over all the vital information to Sardar Patel at Delhi and J D Nagarwala, the then CID chief who was appointed the Investigating Officer to probe into the murder conspiracy. Nagarwala's submission confirmed that he had kept the then Home Minister apprised of the minute details of the investigations and Desai was satisfied with his move.

J D Nagarwala received a severe reprimand from the Commission as soon as the fact surfaced that the first entry about the Gandhi murder conspiracy was made into the Crime Report No 1 of the Special Branch, CID only on 31 January 1948 though the then Home Minister's oath confirmed that Nagarwala had started probing immediately after the information received from Prof Jain, which was passed over to the Special Branch, CID on 21 January 1948. Prof Jain was, however, contacted for the first time only on 17 February 1948, almost after a month when he had exposed the vital clues. Special Branch records blatantly showed that there was no endeavour made to contact source either at Ahmednagar or Poona counterparts, and CID activities were confined only to surveillance of a chosen few suspects in Bombay and that too had yielded no subsequent leads at all.

When Madanlal was remanded in the custody of Delhi Police, he had made revelations (20/24 January 1948) about the conspiracy and vivid descriptions of Vishnu R Karkare and Nathuram V Godse. Madanlal's statements were brought to Bombay on 27 January 1948 by U H Rana, the then Deputy Inspector General of Police.

Karkare had an arrest warrant already issued against him in the previous year for subversive activities and his name also featured in the murder plot conveyed by Prof Jain, yet Crime Records did not show any substantial or tangible move to apprehend him. Karkare and Apte were arrested only on 14 February 1948, 14 days after the great tragedy. Deposing before the Commission, N M Kamte, the then Inspector General of Police, Maharashtra under whose jurisdiction the entire conspiracy fell stated to have been kept in complete dark.[21] All these Special Branch daily rosters were, however, routinely scrutinised by the then Home Minister, Morarji Desai!

In the Commission of Inquiry, Justice Kapur only upheld the observations of Justice Amta Charan, Special Judge in the murder trial, stating that the period between 21 and 30 January 1948 was the most crucial and 'there was utter lack of cooperative effort in the province of Bombay Police and between the Bombay and Delhi Police'.[22] R N Banerjee (ICS), the then Union Home Secretary, deposing before the Kapur Commission, exploded a bomb-shell by revealing that he came to know of any conspiracy angle to the tragedy only on 31 January 1948 at the bungalow of Sardar Patel while attending an informal condolence meet for the late Mahatma. Banerjee was harshly critical of Sanjevi who being the Director, Intelligence Branch and the Inspector General of Police, Delhi was obliged to keep Banerjee, the then Home Secretary apprised of the conspiracy in details and seek his advice in regard to coordinating with Bombay Police.[23] Sardar Patel had left this world way back in 1950. Should he have faced the Commission, nobody knew what was there in store for the then Home Minister of India who was in charge of the Gandhi Murder Conspiracy.

༄

My long lasting regrets

I know that I would not live long. I have reached the fag end of my life. For the last forty years I have been remorseful for not being able to save my beloved leader, the leader of the Nation, Mahatmaji.

Even now at times, I do get up at midnight with the harrowing memory of the humiliation faced at the then Bombay Premier's Bungalow.

'You are one of the conspirators. You have been helping Madanlal. I will have you locked up.'

Morarji Desai's words keep ringing in my ears even today. Being an ardent follower of Bapu, I wanted to save his life when Madanlal made an abortive attempt on his life. Risking my life at the hands of the Hindu extremists, I had volunteered to offer, ignoring, of course, my family and my little child had started crawling then, my services for the nation. Was it my fault to try to save the life of the 'Father of the Nation'?

Was it meaningless whatever we were taught when imprisoned during the 'Quit India Movement' in 1942?

More than forty years have gone by. After the trial at the Red Fort, the appeal at the High Court, an inquiry commission was set up fifteen years after the heinous crime, so much research went into unearth the psyche behind the gruesome killing, yet I do still firmly believe that we could have saved the apostle of non-violence from the brutal death.

On 5 January 1948, Madanlal was kept under overnight detention for creating trouble and assaulting the then Congress leader Rao Saheb Patwardhan at Ahmednagar. After preliminary investigation, on 9 January 1948, Inspector Razak had recommended arrest for both Madanlal Pahwa and his mentor, Vishnu Karkare. Due to red-tapism, the arrest warrants were issued after seven days on 12 January 1948 when both the accused were on their way to Delhi to carry out their *mission* with other members in the conspiracy bid.

Madanlal was held again on 18 January 1948 at Delhi when in a pandemonium at a public meeting followed by the speech of Nehru, then Prime Minister, Madanlal dared to touch Indira, the accompanying daughter of Nehru, yet he was let off scot-free.

After the abortive attempt on Bapu on 20 January 1948, Madanlal had divulged vital clues which bore vivid descriptions of Godse and Karkare, his accomplices, yet the Delhi Police while conducting a man-hunt on the same evening did not bother to check the whereabouts of the suspects with Ashutosh Lahiri at the Hindu Mahasabha office.

More surprisingly, after the revelations from Madanlal, the Delhi Police team which had left for Bombay on 20

January 1948 itself for further investigations, in collaboration with the Bombay Police, did not carry even a single page typed confession, albeit partial, and instead took some pieces of papers with barely scribbles on it. Madanlal's detailed confession obtained on 24 January 1948 ran up to 54 typed pages having the details of Godse's Marathi daily with the niceties of both Karkare and Badge, yet there was hardly any attempt made to get to the office of the Hindu Rashtra.

On 24/25 January 1948, U H Rana had a detailed meeting at Delhi with Sanjevi who was spearheading the investigation. Hindu Rashrta office at Poona was earlier put under surveillance for their subversive activities by Rana's watch and ward team, yet nobody would ever know why Rana chose not to issue any instruction to raid the office of the Marathi daily. Nobody would ever know instead of flying, after his meeting with Sanjevi, why Rana chose a long train taking almost 36 hours feom Delhi to reach Poona. Rana's office had the photographs of Godse, Apte and Badge yet nobody would know why Rana did not send the photographs of the suspects to Delhi Police who would have ensured entry ban for them at the Birla House on the fateful day of 30 January 1948. Nobody would have any clue as to why Ahmednagar Police had never bothered to check why Badge, an arms peddler having more than 37 arrest warrants pending to his credit had suddenly disappeared. Nobody would ever know why the same Ahmednagar Police never followed up the arrest warrant issued against Karkare on 12 January 1948.

On 9 July 1947, Nathuram Godse had written the following declamatory message in the *Hindu Rashtra* (rechristened from *Agrani*)—he himself was the editor of this Marathi daily. Being the protagonist of Hindutva and an ardent critic of Gandhiji, he wrote:

'Brothers! Our mother land has been cut into pieces. The eagles have torn her skin into bits. Hindu women are being raped in the middle of the road. How long can we tolerate this? It's a shame that lakhs of Hindus live like refugees in their own country. Women being raped burn my heart'. Godse warned Gandhiji, 'Gandhiji! By approving the Pakistan partition, you have stabbed the nation. Unless you change your activities, you must face harsh consequences. We consider the dividers of our nation as traitors of our nation.'

Yet, there was no action taken by Rana's office which had withdrawn the surveillance at the Marathi daily in May 1947!

J D Nagarwala, being the Chief Investigating Officer at Bombay, was convinced that 'Savarkar was at the back of the conspiracy and that he was feigning illness.' Nagarwala's letter of 31 January 1948, the day after the assassination, categorically stated on the strength of what Savarkar's close aides—Appa Ramachandra Kasar, his bodyguard, and Gajanan Vishnu Damle, his secretary disclosed to him that Savarkar, Godse and Apte had met for 40 minutes 'on the eve of their departure to Delhi' and that these two had 'access to the house of Savarkar without any restriction.' In short, Godse and Apte had met Savarkar again, in the absence of Badge, and in addition to their meetings on 14 and 17 January 1948.

Badge's version in the court was that on 17 January 1948 he had gone with the assassin, Nathuram Vinayak

Godse, and their accomplice, Narayan Apte, to Savarkar's home and that he heard Savarkar, while bidding them farewell, say, 'Yashasvi houn ya' (Be successful and come back). On the way back, Apte told Badge that Savarkar had predicted that 'Gandhiji's 100 years were over—there was no doubt that he would be successfully finished.'

I have always asked myself, and this, perhaps I would continue till my dying breath,

'If Nagarwala knew the involvement of Savarkar, why his close aides—Appa Ramachandra Kasar, his bodyguard, and Gajanan Vishnu Damle, his secretary were not examined in the court?'

Why had Sardar Patel, despite being a successful UK qualified lawyer and who, in consultation with Morarji Desai, 'kept [him]self almost in daily touch with the progress of the investigations regarding Bapu's assassination case devoting a large part of his evenings to discussing with Sanjevi the day's progress and giving instructions to him on any points,'[24] failed to advise the prosecution team to produce either Appa Ramachandra Kasar or Gajanan Vishnu Damle to nail Savarkar?

Sanjevi had come to know from Madanlal's confession about the involvement of the Marathi Daily people of Poona in the attack on Bapu made on 20 January 1948. Without much effort, sitting in Delhi itself, Sanjevi could have easily obtained all the necessary details of the Hindu Rasthra even by making a phone call to the Indian Newspaper Society office at Delhi, yet Sanjevi never bothered to exercise his option! We would never know if Sanjevi had developed his lackadaisical approach in the whole episode following his mentor, Sardar Patel who had preferred to proceed to Bombay when Bapu was about to start his last 'fast unto death' on 13 January 1948!

Even after 40 years, there is still ambivalence if Nathuram V Godse who saw himself as a passionate and ardent defender of the Hindu motherland against the depredations of Muslims, was a member of the RSS. Nathuram, as general consensus appears, was an active member of the RSS and had left the organisation in the thirties to become a Mahasabha sympathiser.

At the time of the brutal attack on Gandhiji, whether Godse formally remained a member of the RSS is much less important than the fact that though the Hindu Mahasabha and the RSS had some ideological differences, both organisations were united in their extreme hostility to Gandhi as well as to Muslims. Madhav Sadashiv Golwalkar and Veer Savarkar shared a platform in Poona in 1952, as Sitaram Yechury's *What Is This Hindu Rashtra* (Madras: Frontline Publications, 1993) has recently documented.

In the last five decades following Gandhi's assassination, the RSS cleverly argued that Godse had no association with the organisation, and curiously Nathuram's younger brother, Gopal Godse, who was convicted of partaking in the conspiracy to murder Gandhi and served a fifteen-year jail term and still speaks in the most bitter terms of Gandhi as the betrayer of India, has himself on more than one occasion had to issue strong rejoinders to the RSS, with whose ideological outlook he is otherwise in complete sympathy, for attempting to disguise his brother's long-term association with the RSS.

Only the other day, I was flipping through the pages of a news magazine, the usual routine I would normally follow in the afternoons, when my eyes stuck to an interview of Gopal Godse captured in *The Outlook*. Shortly after releasing Godse's book, *Why I Assassinated Mahatma Gandhi*, in December 1993, Gopal Godse in the interview stated: 'All the [Godse] brothers were in the RSS. Nathuram, Dattatreya, myself and Govind. You can say we grew up in the RSS rather than in our home. It was like a family to us. Nathuram had become a baudhik karyavah [intellectual worker] in the RSS. He has said in his statement that he left the RSS. He said it because [Madhav Sadashiv] Golwalkar and the RSS were in a lot of trouble after the murder of Gandhi. But he did not leave the RSS.'[25]

I know I would never get the answer why during his long prosecution argument C K Daphtary, as the Chief Public Prosecutor, did not involve RSS at all in the trial; the prosecution did not even hint, much less prove even the remotest connection of RSS with the murder of the Mahathma, and thus RSS is not blamed anywhere in the judgement delivered in the case. Is it due to any invisible string being pulled by those influential 'authorities' who even having known the conspiracy well in advance, preferred to sit idle with their mouth shut? Perhaps, the generation next might have the zeal in unearthing what is hitherto not made known.

It was in March 1948, I distinctly remember, about a month after Mahatmaji was brutally assassinated, I was feeling at a loss. How would I safeguard the truth and make it known to the common people? In order to avert the national tragedy, I had passed over all the information to the highest authorities on 21 January 1948, yet it was only on 17 February 1948, after a couple of weeks we had lost the 'Father of the Nation', that a Police officer came to record my statement for post-mortem investigation.

Pandit Nehru, the then Prime Minister of India, would visit Bombay in April 1948, as I had gathered, to attend the All India Congress Committee meeting. 'Is it possible to meet Panditji and apprise him of everything?'—I was asking myself. 'Perhaps not. Who would arrange for my appointment? At least, I should handover a letter addressed to the Prime Minister.'—I was trying to comfort myself.

It was, however, more difficult than what I had anticipated. I was literally pushed from pillar to post seeking an interview, and ultimately, at the behest of some of the United Province Congress functionaries, whom I had known, I had obtained a slip for admission to the Government House to try my luck. Panditji was indeed hard pressed and when he was leaving for Delhi, God willing, I could manage a one-minute slot.

'You have come without an appointment.' the Prime Minister had overtly voiced his displeasure.

'Sir, it's really important and I won't take much of your time.' I had produced my letter.

I had seen him going towards his car with the letter in hand. In the car too he had been going through my letter. I hoped that something would happen; now, the world would come to know about the heinous conspiracy of the century. No, it was my mistake, yet again. I never received an acknowledgement.

Annexure 1

28 Shivaji Park
Bombay 28

20 April 1948

To
Pandit Jawaharlal Nehru
Prime Minister of India
Delhi

My Dear Panditji,

It is with deep regret and overwhelming sorrow that I bring
to your kind notice certain events that took place before and
after the assassination of Mahatma Gandhi, whose life I tried
to save by my interview with the Hon'ble Mr B G Kher and
Hon'ble Mr Morarji Desai, the Premier and the Home Minister
of the Government of Bombay, respectively. As a matter of fact,
I wanted to address this letter to you long back, but thinking
whether it would reach you, and whether you would be able
to spare time to go through it, I abstained from posting it.

The events which I wanted to bring to your notice are as
follows:

As soon as I read in the papers of 21 January 1948 about
the dastardly attack on Mahatmaji's life by one Madanlal,
because of certain things I knew about Madanlal, I immediately
tried to contact Sardar Vallabhbhai Patel who happened to be
in Bombay at that time. On being told that he had already left,
I rang up Mr S K Patil, President of the BPCC, but I learned
that he had gone to the aerodrome to see the Sardar off. Then
on telephone I contacted Mr B G Kher, the Premier of Bombay,
and asked for an interview. I met the Premier and the Home
Minister at 4.00 pm the same day at the Secretariat and related

to them the immediate past history of Madanlal with all details known to me.

Madanlal was introduced to me as a refugee from the Punjab who needed some employment. In order to help him to earn a living, I gave him to sell some of my books on commission basis for sometime. Later on, after a few days, when he met me, he said that he had opened a fruit shop in Ahmednagar, where he was getting on well. One day, in the course of his conversation, he revealed that he was helped in Ahmednagar by one Karkare (who is today one of the main accused in the case against Godse), he had tried to assault Rao Saheb Patwardhan in Ahmednagar while he was addressing a meeting preaching Hindu-Muslim unity, that he had tried to dynamite the house of a local rich Muslim, that there was a dump of arms in Ahmednagar, that the local police was communal-minded and hence there was no question of any action being taken against him and his colleagues (some of these items of news had appeared in the Marathi papers, also, which were shown to me by Madanlal).

Madanlal said that after hearing about his adventures in Ahmednagar, Veer Savarkar of the Hindu Mahasabha had sent for him and patted him on his back for his anti-Muslim activities in Ahmednagar. He also revealed that there was a conspiracy to murder Mahatma Gandhi, and that the information regarding the movements of Gandhiji, was conveyed to him and his party by a Maharashtrian lady who was a member of 'Gandhiji's entourage. He also gave me information about another big dump of arms in Bombay-guarded by a Maharashtrian disguised as a Sikh.

When Madanlal talked to me about the above conspiracy, I remonstrated with him and condemned the diabolical idea in the strongest terms and warned him to remove even the thought of such a heinous crime from his mind, l also tried to rouse nobler instincts in him and advised him to devote his time to some constructive and peaceful work. At that time Madanlal actually promised me to disassociate himself with all communal activities and said that because of the help I had given to him in his hour of greatest distress, he regarded me as his father and would never do anything against my wishes.

Otherwise also, as of late, it has become a habit with the refugees and other anti-social people to talk of communal violence and crime, hence, in reality, I could not even dream that there could be some truth in the mischievous intentions of Madanlal.

But the bomb attempt by Madanlal on Mahatmaji's life at Delhi gave an extremely rude shock to me. I hastened to inform the Premier and the Home Minister of the Bombay Government, whatever I knew about this matter as a result of my talk with Madanlal. I tried to bring to their notice that the bomb explosion at Delhi should not be treated lightly or cursorily as a mere attempt of creating chaos at the prayer-meeting; it appeared to be a cruel and deliberate attempt on the part of some of the members of the Hindu community to remove Mahatmaji from our midst. I reported to the ministers the conversation in full details I had with Madanlal and tried to impress upon them what now I had begun to feel that the act of throwing a bomb on Mahatmaji was not the work of a mad man; it appeared to be a concerted effort of the Hindu Mahasabha and the RSS to murder him with the help of some hired dare-devils from amongst the aggrieved refugees. I urged upon the ministers that it was absolutely necessary to take the strictest and the most immediate safety measures to save Mahatmaji's life. I also offered my services to help the Government in all possible ways. I told them that I was willing to fly to Delhi if necessary and meet Madanlal for the purpose of unearthing the satanic conspiracy. I also mentioned several other names and the information about the dump of arms in Bombay which had been given to me by Madanlal.

After hearing my story, the ministers assured me that all necessary precautions will be taken to safeguard Mahatmaji's life and that Sardar Patel, Home Minister of the Central Government, would be immediately informed.

I do not know what happened afterwards, nor did I hear anything from the ministers.

Suddenly, on 30 January 1948 the news of Gandhiji's assassination struck the country like lightning. It is now useless to describe the feelings of shame, sorrow and remorse with which I was filled like the rest of my countrymen.

However, I again contacted Mr Kher and Mr Desai and told them how grieved I was, when nothing could he done in spite of my giving the information. If proper measures had been taken perhaps the great catastrophe could be averted and the life of the Father of our Nation could be saved. When I finished saying these things, Mr Kher agreed with me and said, 'Yes, perhaps we are guilty, and probably Gandhiji's life could have been saved if we had acted more appropriately.'

Just then, Mr Morarji Desai happened to come there. Kher Saheb told him what I had said, and to my utmost surprise, without exchanging a word with me, he started shouting at the top of his voice and threatened me by saying, 'You are one of the conspirators. You have helped Madanlal and that is why you did not inform us before hand, and now you have the audacity to blame us. You should be put under arrest.' I was shocked to see Mr B G Kher also joining the Home Minister in charging me of having a part in the criminal conspiracy to murder Mahatmaji. I do not know whether the ministers were serious in their charges, or whether they were only threatening me to shut my mouth. I must confess that it was the rudest shock they could give me. I, however, tried my best to keep cool and simply said that if this was the reward I should get for my attempt to save the life of the Father of the Nation, I was prepared to undergo any punishment they would give me. I protested that jail could not terrify me, as I had been in jail in the Movement of 1942. Hence if they wanted to imprison me they could get me arrested then and there. They would not have to bother even to send the police, as I had presented myself before them. But, I further told them that I never expected such an attitude or behaviour from responsible political and Government leaders of their eminence. Afterwards the Home Minister cooled down and said that he did not want to get me arrested, as he knew that I was innocent. If he wanted to send me to jail he could have done it earlier, and it was very wrong on my part even to suggest that the Government had not done everything possible to protect Gandhiji's life.

I left the matter there, only reminding the Minister (Mr Desai) about the dumps of arms and ammunition about which I had previously intimated to him and which to my knowledge had not been unearthed. I also reminded him of the names I had given to him in my first and subsequent interviews with him.

Now I have heard from the police that I am to be produced in the court on behalf of the Crown. Needless to say, I readily agreed and my statements have already been recorded with all details by the police and the Chief Presidency Magistrate of Bombay. The Presidency Magistrate took it down my full statement, which the police refused to do and I expect that it would be of some help in bringing the guilty persons to book.

Now, the question arises as to why I have written this long letter to you and encroached upon your precious time?

Firstly, 1 want to bring to your notice all the above facts because even now I am unable to get over my feelings that the Ministers of the Government Bombay did not act properly and that if they had done so with urgency and earnestness which the cause demanded, may be, the life of Mahatmaji could be saved.

Secondly, I feel—and I do not think it will be unknown to the Provincial or Central Governments—that the RSS and the Hindu Mahasabhaites are reviving their activities. This news has appeared in the daily press. Now, there are vague and sinister rumours and threats on their parts to make attempts on your life and on the lives of the progressive national leaders. I do not think that such devilish plans, and even actions can be beyond these anti-national elements.

Hence, impelled by a sense of duty, and the great loss which our country his already suffered, I am taking the liberty to address this personal letter to you and hope that not only would it be taken in the same light, but would also receive due consideration.

Once again I pledge my services to you and to the cause of uprooting the enemies of the people.

I shall anxiously expect to hear from you and I hope you will spare a few minutes and send me a word in reply, which would satisfy me.

With kindest regards, I remain,

Yours sincerely,

J C Jain

(Dr Jagdishchandra Jain)

Notes

1. *National Herald,* 30 July 1946
2. Pyrelal: *Mahatma Gandhi—The Last Phrase* p.254
3. Units must have right to secede Joshi's memorandum to the Cabinet Mission: *The Pioneer,* 18 April 1946
4. *Hindustan Standard,* 1 September 1946
5. *The Tribune,* 14 May 1947
6. Pyrelal: *Mahatma Gandhi—The Last Phrase,* pp.296-7
7. Pyrelal: *Mahatma Gandhi—The Last Phrase,* p.389
8. Richard Hough: *Mountbatten, Hero of Our Time,* p.290
9. Menon: *Transfer of Power in India* p.385
10. Azad: *India Wins Freedom,* p.198
11. Sardar Patel's letter to Gandhiji, 24 August 1947
12. Pyrelal: *Mahatma Gandhi—The Last Phrase* pp.705-731
13. Pyrelal: *Mahatma Gandhi—The Last Phase* p.756
14. Durga Das (ed.): *Sardar Patel's Correspondence (1945-50),* Vol 6, p.56
15. Jawaharlal Nehru: *Independence and After (1946-49)* p.17
16. *The Hindustan Times,* 3 February 1948
17. *Indian Express,* 29 January 1948
18. Durga Das (ed.): *Sardar Patel's Correspondence (1945-50),* Vol 6, p.55
19. Report of Commission of Inquiry into the Conspiracy to Murder Mahatma Gandhi, Part 1, p.61
20. Report of Commission of Inquiry into Conspiracy to Murder Mahatma Gandhi Part II, XXVI, p.343
21. Report of Commission of Inquiry into Conspiracy to Murder Mahatma Gandhi Part II, p.210
22. Report of Commission of Inquiry into Conspiracy to Murder Mahatma Gandhi Part II, p.351
23. R K Nigam, Ed: *Memoirs of Old Mandarins of India: The Administrative Change as the ICS Administrators Saw In India,* 1984
24. Letter to Nehru dated 27 February 1948 Durga Das (ed.), *Sardar Patel's Correspondence (1945-50)*
25. *The Outlook:* 28 January 1994

Glossary

Agrani	A Marathi (local language) daily from Poona, India, launched on 28 March 1944, by Nathuram V Godse and Narayan Apte to propagate the cause of the Hindu organisation
Ahimsa	The principle of non-violence, which Gandhiji considered as one of the highest moral values to live by
Ashokan wheel	The wheel on the Indian National Flag designed after a wheel on a column set up by the Emperor Ashoka
Bandh	General strike when public life comes to a standstill
Bapu	Father, used as a form of address; a name by which Gandhiji is often affectionately referred to
Bhawan	A building for a special purpose
BPCC	Bombay Provincial Congress Party
Brahmin	Hindu of the highest caste
Burqa	Veil
Chaprasi	A person whose job is to look after the entrance of a building or carry messages
Chitpawan Brahmins	Chitpawan Brahmins are a Brahmin community of Konkan, the coastal region of Western Maharashtra, India, who gained prominence among the sect
Chowk	A road junction or a roundabout
CID	Criminal Investigation Department

Danda	A baton
Darshan	An occasion on which one is permitted to see God's idol or a revered person
Diwali	Hindu New Year, the Festival of Lights
Durga Das	(1900-1974) Editor, Associated Press of India (forerunner of the Press Trust of India), Chief Editor, The Hindustan Times
FIR	First Information Report
Gita	(Bhagavadgita) Sacred book of the Hindus
Goonda	A gangster or criminal
Gurudev	A title of respect offered to Rabindranath Tagore
Himalayas	A mountain range in Asia, separating the Indian subcontinent from the Tibetan Plateau, which includes the planet's highest peaks i.e. Mount Everest and K2.
Hindu Mahasabha	Akhil Bhârat Hindû Mahâsabhâ, a Hindu nationalist organisation, founded in 1915 to counter the Muslim League and the Indian National Congress. V D Savarkar was one of the earlier Presidents of the Mahasabha.
Hindu Rashtra	A Marathi (local language) daily from 'Agrani', Poona, India was subsequently, following a ban, rechristened to the 'Hindu Rashtra' in 1946
Hindu Rashtra Darshan	Hindu nationalist political philosophy
Hindutva	A very strong or aggressive sense of Hindu identity
Guru	A trusted adviser; a mentor
Jihad	A holy war fought by Muslims against who oppose Islam
Lathi	Baton
Maharaj	A title added to the name of a God-Man
Maharashtrian	An Indo-Aryan language, spoken in the Maharashtra region of western India
Mahatma	A deeply spiritual person; a great soul

Manu and Abha	Grand-nieces of Gandhi
Maharashtra Niwas	A sort of a guest house for Maharashtrians
Moslem	Muslim
Pandit	A person with sound knowledge of *Shastras*; Hindu scriptures, or a person knowledgeable in a particular field
Pyarelal	Pyarelal Nayyar (1899-1982) was the Personal Secretary to Mahatma Gandhi in his later years
Quaid-i-Azam	Urdu: Great leader; referred here to Mohammad Ali Jinnah
RSS	Rashtriya Swayamsevak Sangh is a Hindu nationalist, volunteer organisation in India
Sadhu	A holy man
Saheb/Saab	A title added to a person's name to show respect
Sanghachalak	Chief of the organisation, mainly in RSS
Sanghatanist	Organiser
Sardar	Vallabhbhai Patel was often addressed as Sardar which means *Chief* in various Indian languages
Satyagraha	A form of protest, originally introduced by Gandhiji, based on a non-violent approach
Satyavinayak Pooja	An offering to God (in Hindu religion)
Seth	A merchant; a rich man
Shaheed	A martyr
Shishya	A follower of a religious leader or teacher
Sikh	A member of the Sikh religion
Sushila Nayar	(1914-2000) was Gandhi's personal Physician and the younger sister of Pyarelal Nayyar, Personal Secretary to Mahatma Gandhi
Tonga	A two wheeled lightly covered carriage, pulled by a single horse

Index

www.ingramcontent.com/pod-product-compliance
Lightning Source LLC
Chambersburg PA
CBHW051211090426
42740CB00022B/3457